The
Lean IT Field Guide
A Roadmap for Your Transformation

The

Lean IT Field Guide

A Roadmap for Your Transformation

Michael A. Orzen • Thomas A. Paider

CRC Press
Taylor & Francis Group
Boca Raton London New York

CRC Press is an imprint of the
Taylor & Francis Group, an **informa** business

A PRODUCTIVITY PRESS BOOK

CRC Press
Taylor & Francis Group
6000 Broken Sound Parkway NW, Suite 300
Boca Raton, FL 33487-2742

© 2016 by Michael A. Orzen & Thomas A. Paider
CRC Press is an imprint of Taylor & Francis Group, an Informa business

No claim to original U.S. Government works

Printed on acid-free paper
Version Date: 20150909

International Standard Book Number-13: 978-1-4987-3038-9 (Paperback)

Visit the Taylor & Francis Web site at
http://www.taylorandfrancis.com

and the CRC Press Web site at
http://www.crcpress.com

For Lynda, my constant reminder of selfless compassion

M. A. O.

and

For Tara and Ethan, my True North

T. A. P.

Contents

Foreword

From iPhones to electric cars, better, smarter products are the key to revolutionizing society while continuing to give greater autonomy and enjoyment to each individual person. IT is now a critical component of the (hardware, software, service) system that makes a twenty-first century great product; therefore, a leaner IT is vital to developing better products. This field guide hits upon many of the most impactful questions in running a business and provides a clear path to finding your own answers.

Lean is often misunderstood as a toolbox of organizational techniques when it is, in fact, as the authors explain well, both a *learning system* and a *respect system*. For instance, a key idea of lean is that *batches are bad* and *flow is good*, but, more deeply, lean thinking is really about understanding what management *decisions* lead to batching, *why* this introduces *un-levelness* in the process (*mura*), and how it creates unreasonable burdens on either people or systems (*muri*) and results in what waste (*muda*). Lean is the discovery process to understand the reasoning that led to batching in the first place and recognizing the wasteful consequences this has for customers, employees, and shareholders.

Many IT approaches have built upon the insight that *batches are bad* and *continuous flow* is good: agile, scrum, kanban. Although development teams love them, they have so far failed, as a whole, to convince senior management. Like most innovations, having—or even proving—a new idea is not enough: The organization must also develop the capability to work with it to deliver consistently. In effect, this is what kaizen is about: continuously training teams and their managers to improve and change so that they can accept, embrace, and create innovation more easily and, indeed, fight harder to make it work.

With this field guide, Mike and Tom address directly the know-why and know-how needed at the leadership and management levels to support a sustaining transformation within IT and, indeed, the entire enterprise. In this, the guide is absolutely critical to any success with lean in IT because it highlights not just the organizational techniques of more agile and lean processes, but also the leadership work required to help management adopt these new approaches. Lean IT and agile heroes often display an antimanagement feeling that does little to support their cause. Here, Mike and Tom thoughtfully show that management's role is essential to train people daily and support team-level improvement work. Without management involvement, lean IT team victories remain just that—local wins that are rarely spread throughout the IT value chain to effect a true end-to-end transformation.

By clarifying the main definitions; specifying, step by step, the foundational management skills; and providing many examples distinguishing success from setback, Mike and Tom have written a savvy, smart, and mindful guide to your own lean IT transformation. As Mike taught me, "It takes 40 days to make it and another 40 days to own it." This field guide provides a wonderfully written, lucid, succinct guide to what you need to know to succeed.

Michael Ballé
Co-founder, Institut Lean France, Paris

Acknowledgments

In reflecting on the creation of this book, we are awestruck by the generous contribution of so many individuals and organizations. Perhaps the defining feature of the lean community is the willingness to share ideas and help others to learn and understand. Imagine the progress that could be made across the world if everyone was a lean thinker! If when something went wrong we didn't point fingers, we didn't think there is a vast conspiracy out to get us or that the world is rigged, but rather viewed it as an opportunity to investigate, learn, and improve. Instead of assuming the worst in people, we would assume the best; instead of looking from afar and making judgments, we would go and see for ourselves. And while this vision may be far from reality, our experiences and the people we met while writing this book give us hope.

The Lean IT Field Guide is the collective work of many people over many years, only some of whom are named on these pages. To those we have left out inadvertently, the mistake is ours. Any errors in this book are solely those of the authors, not the individuals that have guided us along the way.

Both Mike and Tom would like to thank our tireless reviewers: Jim Benson, Gary Butler, Richard Carroll, Carmen Deardo, Jeff Karl, Beau Keyte, Tanya Lasuk, Whitney Mantonya, Jeromy Markwort, Jason Patterson, Peg Pennington, Robert Slepin, and Kevin Yania. Your patience and attention to detail were amazing.

Many others helped out through conversations and by opening up their organizations to us. Specific thanks to Bruno Guicardi and Felipe Brito of CI&T, Ven Miriyala and Alberto Ruocco of American Electric Power, Elaine Richardson of Export Development Canada, and others who have chosen to remain anonymous. Thanks to Kelsey Chapman of Kelsey Designs (http://www.kelseydesigns.com), who proved that no image was too difficult to produce and no timeline was too tight to meet.

Special thanks to a wonderful group of people at The Ohio State University's Center for Operational Excellence and Masters in Business Operational Excellence program. They are a special group of people with a very worthy purpose: to spread the principles and practices of lean, Six Sigma, and operational excellence. We particularly want to thank Gary Butler for his guidance as a reviewer and advisor, Peg Pennington for her reviews of and contribution to the project (and her humility), and Dr. Peter Ward for his encouragement and vision for the lean community through the highly successful organizations and programs he leads at Ohio State.

Mike would also like to thank the wonderful clients and friends he has known over the past 20 years while striving to better understand and apply lean thinking. In particular, WelchAllyn, Con-way, Nike, Plexus, Gentex Optics, Pacific Northwest Labs, Western Digital, Rovi, Leatherman, Nationwide, Tillamook, and HanesBrands have provided learning opportunities with countless obstacles and occasional breakthroughs in understanding through never-ending practice of PDCA. Special thanks to Michael Ballé, whose friendship and challenge pushed Mike beyond some of his *90s paradigms* and toward something new!

Tom would like to thank many colleagues at Nationwide who offered support and encouragement. Specifically, Guru Vasudeva, CIO, Application and Data Services, who didn't hesitate when asked if he would support the project; and Enterprise CIO Mike Keller for his support of lean IT at Nationwide and willingness to allow the experiments to happen. Too many others to name past and present at Nationwide contributed to this book directly or unknowingly through conversations and their support of the lean journey. Thanks to the Nationwide IT and BTO organizations for supporting the project and for serving as a learning lab by using lean to help create a great experience for associates and to drive incredible value and caring to our customers.

Both Mike and Tom would like to close with a very special thank you to Lynda, Tara, and Ethan. Their love, patience, and guidance during the writing process make this book as much theirs as ours.

Authors

Michael A. Orzen, MBA, has a consulting and coaching career spanning more than 20 years. He received the BA degree in economics from Stanford University and the MBA degree in finance and management from the University of Oregon. He has gathered a unique blend of lean, IT, finance, and operations experience, which he uses to coach organizations in their pursuit of enterprise excellence. His personable approach and people-first philosophy have inspired leaders and empowered workforces to successfully apply conscious awareness, lean, and enterprise excellence practices in many complex work environments.

He is the coauthor of the award-winning book, *Lean IT—Enabling and Sustaining Your Lean Transformation* (CRC Press, 2011), and recipient of the Shingo Research and Professional Publication Award. He holds degrees from Stanford University and the University of Oregon. Mike teaches with the Lean Enterprise Institute, the Shingo Institute, and the Ohio State University Fisher School of Business.

When he's not traveling around the world consulting with clients and sharing his vision of lean and respect for people, as well as using personal awareness to drive excellence, he resides in Oregon City, Oregon, with his wife, Lynda, and pride of cats.

Thomas A. Paider, MBOE, is an IT executive for Nationwide, a Fortune 100 insurance and financial services company. He received his BS degree in business administration from Ohio Dominican University and his master's degree in business operational excellence from the Ohio State University. His teams work across Nationwide to foster lean thinking and improve software development capability. He is also a lean coach in the Masters in Business Operational Excellence program at The Ohio State University.

Tom is the cofounder of the IT Leadership Network at the Center for Operational Excellence at The Ohio State University, a partnership between industry and academic leaders focused on helping member companies collaborate and sustain their lean journeys.

Tom has consulted with dozens of companies, ranging from startups to large enterprises, on their lean transformations. He resides in Hilliard, Ohio, with his wife, Tara, and son, Ethan.

Introduction

When IT stops, the business stops! If you work in any organization, in any industry, for profit or not, you rely on information and the technology to manage, share, analyze, and understand it. Information is the connective tissue that binds our thoughts, our words, and our actions. Without effective communication of actionable information, no organization can function and improve. Less than half a century into the age of the Internet, we have become forever dependent on instant access to information, real-time communication, and the immediate gratification they bring.

As our world continues to experience a progressively accelerating rate of change, we can expect the amount and quality of information, supporting functionality, access, and our reliance on IT to grow exponentially. And here's the tragic news: After half a century of pursuing operational and enterprise excellence through process improvement, lean, Six Sigma, and a vast collection of tools and methodologies, we have barely begun to make headway in applying these practices to IT and the effective management of information. Certainly, there are a few exceptions and we'll explore those organizations and what they are doing to make lean IT work for them, but of the hundreds of companies we have visited throughout the world, very few are successfully driving measurable, sustainable improvement in their IT groups at a level we can describe as *transformative*.

Although there are many books that attempt to address lean IT, agile, lean startup, IT service management, and ITIL, none of these works address the *how to* of actually putting principles, systems, and tools into practice. They do provide a framework from which to think and understand, but they lack a process from which to act. As we reflect on our combined experience in IT, organizational change, and process improvement, which exceeds 30 years, it is clear that a roadmap is needed!

Although we target IT for transformation, the information contained in this book is universally applicable to all organizations and business functions. Created as a field guide, this book differentiates itself in its approach to lean and IT to provide not only learning concepts, but also a guide to practical execution. It will present a clear and definitive methodology on how to start, execute, and sustain a lean IT transformation. This book also creates a rich multimedia experience through a companion website for the reader that includes an illustrated roadmap and downloadable content including tools, templates, and guides, as well as videos that highlight practices at profiled companies. It is intended to be a launching point for the methods and tools needed to undertake a deeply effective, game-changing, and lasting lean IT transformation.

 Whenever you see this icon, please refer to our website at LeanITField Guide.com for additional resources. Please share your comments and feedback to let us know how we can make the site even better!

In the pages that follow, we will explore the following key topics to position you for successful transformation of your IT group:

- "Lean Primer for IT Professionals"—level-set the conversation
- "The Transformation Framework"—see the path
- "The Importance of Purpose"—begin with the end in mind
- "Day Zero"—let's get started
- "The Paradox of Process"—constructive tension
- "Problem-Solving Scientists"—deliberately thinking about learning
- "Everything Is Visible"—now we all see
- "Why Management (Still) Matters"—the secret sauce
- "Sustain Your Progress"—the essential (and most elusive) element
- "The Importance of Strategic Alignment"—aligning effort
- "Engineering Excellence"—effective creativity
- "Continue the Journey"—stand back and see the whole

Whether you are the CIO of a multinational corporation, IT professional, leader of continuous improvement, or in need of a fully engaged and aligned IT group in your organization, this book is for you. It is our hope that the roadmap we share will lead you and your organization toward operational excellence within and beyond your IT department, where everyone's work is enabled and made easier through a more responsive, effective, and value-driven information technology team. We wish you deep learning, discovery, and sustained success on your lean IT journey.

Let's get started!

Chapter 1

Lean Primer for IT Professionals

> The most exciting breakthroughs of the 21st century will not occur
> because of technology, but because of an expanded concept of
> what it means to be human.
>
> **John Naisbitt**[1]
> *Megatrends: Ten New Directions Transforming*
> *Our Lives, August 16, 1988*

Introduction

The purpose of this chapter is to provide the reader with some familiarity on various applications of lean to IT. It's important to have a basic understanding of fundamental concepts and areas of practice in order to stay grounded in principles that really provide lasting results. We often see IT organizations jump from hot new topic to hot new topic, applying a *flavor of the month* strategy that never sustains itself.

There have been many great books that cover the fundamental concepts of lean, Six Sigma, and continuous process improvement; our intent is not to rehash that information (that wouldn't be very lean at all). In the past, most of the books on lean were oriented toward manufacturing. That all changed around the year 2000 when the world saw a widening application of lean into areas including healthcare, service industries, product development, education, government, and our favorite topic: lean IT.

In 2010, Mike coauthored the book, *Lean IT—Enabling and Sustaining Your Lean Transformation,*[2] which received a Shingo Research and Publication Award. Chapter 2 of the book, "Foundations of Lean," has been widely used by IT and non-IT groups as a brief primer explaining many of the core concepts while placing them within the context of information management and technology. This reading will give you a conceptual overview of lean within an IT context.

We encourage you to download Chapter 2 of *Lean IT* and find additional resources at LeanITFieldGuide.com.

The Lean IT Cosmos

We use the term *lean IT* to refer to all applications of lean thinking, principles, methods, and tools in the world of information management, communication, and technology. There are numerous applications of lean in the IT field including software development, operations, infrastructure, and project management, to name a few. All of these approaches demonstrate the effectiveness and applicability of lean thinking to information technology. The clearer your understanding of these components, the more effective you will be at applying the tools and methods needed to achieve your specific objectives.

Agile/Lean Software Development

Many of the people in companies we work with seem to equate lean IT to agile. While agile effectively applies many of the core principles of lean, it uses only a subset of lean techniques and targets the software development process. We see lean IT as being much broader.

In 2001, a group of software developers introduced the Agile Manifesto[3] to evangelize short cycles of productivity, giving end users frequent releases of usable software with the express purpose of moving away from traditional overburdening bureaucratic development practices (e.g., Waterfall and Big Bang[4]). The concept of using *small batch sizes* had been introduced in lean manufacturing 50 years earlier, but this was totally new to the world of software development. When the Agile Manifesto was first published, some rejected it as pure fantasy!

The Agile Manifesto proclaims 12 key principles:

1. Our highest priority is to satisfy the customer through early and continuous delivery of valuable software.
2. Welcome changing requirements, even late in development. Agile processes harness change for the customer's competitive advantage.
3. Deliver working software frequently, from a couple of weeks to a couple of months, with a preference to the shorter timescale.
4. Business people and developers must work together daily throughout the project.
5. Build projects around motivated individuals. Give them the environment and support they need, and trust them to get the job done.
6. The most efficient and effective method of conveying information to and within a development team is face-to-face conversation.
7. Working software is the primary measure of progress.
8. Agile processes promote sustainable development. The sponsors, developers, and users should be able to maintain a constant pace indefinitely.
9. Continuous attention to technical excellence and good design enhances agility.
10. Simplicity—the art of maximizing the amount of work not done—is essential.
11. The best architectures, requirements, and designs emerge from self-organizing teams.
12. At regular intervals, the team reflects on how to become more effective, then tunes and adjusts its behavior accordingly.

The core characteristics of agile are short, rapid cycles of work (sprints), business involvement throughout the development process (product owner), team collaboration and self-direction (daily Scrum), visual management (work-in-progress boards and burn-down charts), and reflection (retrospectives, feedback loops, ongoing process improvement), as well as an emphasis on software engineering excellence.

As organizations experimented with agile and Scrum,[5] they discovered that exclusively focusing on software development without considering upstream and downstream operations severely limits the benefits. For example, when agile methods are applied to infrastructure, it often creates a more nimble and flexible infrastructure capability throughout public or private clouds with virtualized servers, storage, and networks. Agile infrastructure also applies many of the same core ideas of faster iterations, small lot sizes, self-directed teams, and kanban.

Kanban

Kanban is a tool originally developed more than 50 years ago to support the Toyota Production System *Just-in-Time* method of making only what is needed, when it is needed, and in the precise amount needed. Kanban (often a physical card) can simply be thought of as an authorization to produce and replenish parts that have been used. Over the years it has been adapted to many uses in manufacturing, service, and knowledge industries.

Kanban, as the term is used in IT, is a visual display board used to (a) visualize the flow of work, (b) limit work-in-process, (c) drive productivity through an awareness of what people are actually working on, and (d) continuously improve the process!

David Anderson[6] introduced the Kanban Method in 2003. Anderson focused on six key elements of using kanban effectively:

1. *Visualize*—The work in IT (and most knowledge work) is essentially invisible. There are no piles of half-finished work sitting around on the factory floor. Kanban exposes the flow of work (or lack of it)—being able to see the flow of work is essential to managing it! Without a clear understanding of what the work is, managing its flow effectively is nearly impossible.

2. *Limit work-in-process (WIP)*—The amount of potential work that is released to be actually worked on is limited based on available capacity. Most IT shops work under the *infinite capacity* model[7] of work management—basically saying *yes we can do that* and beginning work without regard to what is already in flight and what resources are available. Kanban uses a pull system to regulate the release of new work into the work stream. By limiting work-in-process, we only begin new work when work already released is completed or on hold pending some resolution. Work changing status from *in process* to *done* (or *on hold*) signals available capacity and creates a pull signal that additional work can be started.

3. *Manage work flow*—When work stops, bottlenecks can be addressed immediately and countermeasures can be put into place to re-establish the smooth flow of work. The flow of work through each stage of the process is actively monitored and managed.

4. *Make policies clear*—An unambiguous understanding and visualization of how the work flows through the system (based on facts) enables teams to move to a more cogent and objective dialogue of work flow problems and obstacles.
5. *Implement feedback loops*—Teams evaluate what is working and what is not (based on objective measurements which are under their control), feeding this information back as they identify the next step to move toward the higher levels of performance.
6. *Improve collaboratively*—Kanban provides teams with a shared understanding of what the work is, how the work flows, and their current state. With this understanding, teams are much more likely to build consensus around current challenges and countermeasures to address them.

Continuous Delivery

Continuous Delivery (or Continuous Deployment) is all about releasing functional software more frequently and in small chunks. This applies to companies that actually sell software (think Intuit) as well as companies who rely on software to deliver products and services (think Amazon). Continuous delivery (CD) leverages automation, recurrent releases of code, testing at every stage of the process, and a pull-based work flow that permits only successful releases to move to the next stage in the release cycle.

In 2010, Jez Humble and David Farley came out with *Continuous Delivery*[8] and articulated work practices around automation of the build–deploy–test process and supporting collaboration of development teams. Humble passionately explains Continuous Delivery with his mantra, "Reduce the cost, time, and risk of delivering incremental changes to users!" Here again is a clear application of lean thinking: smaller lot sizes, frequent releases, automation to drive quality, shorter time to market, faster feedback cycles of learning, and an emphasis on delivering value to the customer in terms of working software (as opposed to delivering new features).

The benefits of CD go way beyond releasing functional software and include faster reaction time to market changes and surprises, more flexible release options, and a standard of production quality code with every commit. Moving to continuous delivery necessitates a significant building of infrastructure in a software architecture context as well as operationally. But once accomplished, it provides the business with more flexibility of how it delivers new functionality.

Lean Startup

It is estimated by Harvard Business School's Shikhar Ghosh[9] that 75% of all startups fail! Steve Blank developed Lean Startup[10] and Eric Ries popularized it in 2011 with his highly readable book, *The Lean Startup*.[11] The Lean Startup movement applies many of the essential ideas of lean to—you guessed it—conceiving and creating a successful business startup!

Lean Startup is a beautiful example of the Plan–Do–Check–Adjust learning cycle that lies at the root of lean thinking. The approach (described as Build–Measure–Learn) is based on building a set of hypotheses and identifying ways to test them as quickly and cheaply as possible.

In order for Lean Startup to be effective, a key concept known as *Voice of the Customer* plays a central role. Instead of the business deciding what customers want, and then secretly developing a finished product to be introduced to the market with the hope that interest (and sales) will be massive, a learn-as-we-go approach is applied which relies on frequent feedback from prospective customers early and throughout the entire product development process.

This approach fast-tracks learning in order to understand what prospective users actually want and are willing to buy, allowing assumptions to be tested as quickly and cheaply as possible by releasing minimum viable products (MVPs) to prove or disprove assumptions on what customers need and want. This significantly reduces wasted effort, time, and money by limiting work done on features and products customers don't want.

The traditional Business Plan is fading in many business sectors as the rate of change and degree of competition have grown exponentially in recent years. This is particularly true in companies that rely on innovation to create competitive advantage. Lean Startup is all about *failing fast* in order to continually accelerate learning. This means releasing less-than-fully-functioning prototypes (only what is needed to test assumptions) with which to gather feedback from your target market.

Lean Startup significantly reduces the barriers to entry and the cost of failure since small, iterative tests of assumptions allow crucial course corrections (called pivots) early in the process. It is efficiently *discovering* the right business model rather than creating a full-blown but unsubstantiated business model that *achieves ultimate failure*. The focus is on speed, validated learning, customer-driven product development, a flat organization, and agile development.

We are fascinated to see how this community has exploded into an international phenomenon, with Startup Weekends[12] (typically Friday evening,

Saturday/Sunday affairs) occurring around the world. These events are open to anyone who is interested in launching a product. Attendees learn Startup basics and test their hypotheses over the course of the event. On the first evening, attendees give 2-minute pitches, vote on the best ideas, and then work in teams over the weekend applying Lean Startup methods, launching early tests of their concepts. On the final afternoon, attendees present their results to business leaders (and hopefully round-one funders) who critique the project and give valuable feedback on next steps.

DevOps

DevOps is more of a movement than a methodology.[13] The objective is to create a seamless flow of value from IT by coordinating and integrating the activities of Development (Dev), Operations (Ops), and beyond. The concept of a *value stream* has been applied in lean (both in Service and Manufacturing environments) for decades. DevOps leverages many of the lean tools we apply in this book. In *The Phoenix Project*,[14] Gene Kim, Kevin Behr, and George Spafford share a wonderfully illustrative novel, which lays out a general application of DevOps.

Mike had the opportunity to work with one of the authors of *The Phoenix Project*, Gene Kim, and help develop the three insights included in the book. Gene calls these the *3 Ways*.[15] The 3 Ways represent the core principles of DevOps and have sparked a great deal of conversation and debate. Lean practitioners will recognize these as key components of lean thinking[16] and The Toyota Way[17]:

1. *Apply systems thinking*—appreciating and understanding the interdependent nature of the parts of business systems and how they interact with their environment and influence each other. The focus is on the interactions between the Dev and Ops groups and its impact on the uninterrupted flow of value from concept, to development, to release, to service, to maintenance, to upgrade, and eventually to retirement. DevOps places a key emphasis on breaking the silo-based barriers that have traditionally segregated these activities.
2. *Amplify feedback loops among stakeholders*—almost all system-level improvement is reliant on feedback from customers and suppliers. Without feedback (both positive and critical), there is very little check/ adjust activity to continuously improve. In IT, we often see a lack of collaboration from internal IT staff (think Dev to Ops) as well as from end

users. This leaves people assuming that everything is working well or that the other parties don't care enough about the problem to communicate. Both suppositions are often wrong and lead to costly outcomes!

3. *Create a culture of continual experimentation and learning*—learning based on trial and discovery is the bedrock of improvement. To master something is to understand it at each progressively deeper level. DevOps stresses collaboration and fact-based experimentation as the means to build a culture of continuous improvement. Taking risks assumes a new meaning, in that experiments are run using a formalized thoroughness that leads to true learning. That learning is applied to the way work gets done (more about this in Chapter 6).

Lean Project Management

Mike first wrote about Lean Project Management in *Lean IT—Enabling and Sustaining Your Lean Transformation.*[18] He found that much has been written on applying agile (Scrum) methods to project management,[19] but less has been shared on how project managers can apply core lean concepts to their work practices. This topic is essential because so much of what we do in the world of IT revolves around effective project execution—the purview, the *raison d'etre* of project managers.

Most project managers have formed their understanding of project management practice through on-the-job experience and some form of formal education and/or certification. By far, the most common source is the Project Management Institute (PMI).[20] At the time of this writing, PMI offers many project management certifications ranging from *Project Management Professional* to *Agile Certified Practitioner.* There is no lack of information in PMI's collection of project management *best practices.*[21] That being said, we find that the majority of practices concentrate on prediction and control and are not conducive to lean thinking and behavior. We believe planning activities often facilitated by project managers are critical; however, they often devolve to a level of granularity that is neither possible nor helpful. Project managers often struggle with knowing when, where, and how to flex the plan.

In 2012, the PMI introduced a new certification, Agile Certified Practitioner, in response to the huge demand for knowledge on how to apply agile tools and practices to project management. The training was a response to the firmly established Certified Scrum Master training offered through the Scrum Alliance[22] and added an experience requirement (1500 hours working on agile project teams or with agile methodologies) to distinguish itself from the latter. Many resources are available online and from both organizations to compare the two certifications.[23]

Control versus Discovery

As we will explore in detail, the essence of all lean thinking is fact-based discovery and conscious adjustment (check/adjust) based on the reality of the current situation. Traditional project management emphasizes the execution of a fixed project plan. A colleague pointed out that a fixed project plan might actually be a symptom of fixed constraints around the plan that lead to a reluctance to flex as discoveries are made. What may be fixed are our goals, measures, and expected results (and possibly our reluctance to bringing the customer along when new things are discovered).

Of course, there is no way to know precisely what steps will be required to complete a journey when the journey has never been taken.[24] Lean project management emphasizes the power of discovery and anticipates that project schedules and deliverables *must* change based on the real-time learning taking place as the work is done.

The centerpiece of most projects is the project plan—often a Gantt chart, which attempts to identify all the steps that need to be accomplished in order to deliver the project on time, on budget, and with the promised results. Project plans can tend to take on a life of their own as 1000+ line spreadsheets are only viewed by project managers. In fact, a great deal of time is invested (some would say wasted) gathering status updates and updating schedules. In terms of lean, much of this activity is non-value-added work![25]

At the heart of lean is team-based problem solving and learning through experimentation. Instead of project managers enforcing standard practices on running a project (status reports, time sheets, percentage completion estimates, etc.), the focus shifts to enabling active and rapid learning cycles. Notice a common theme here? Learn-as-you-go is a central theme in agile development, kanban, continuous delivery, lean startup, DevOps, and all things lean!

Agile Project Management

The focus on applying agile techniques to project management practices is well and good, but there is perhaps an even more impactful use of lean thinking when it comes to project management practices: the role of the project manager as lean coach and value stream advocate. As agile techniques have proven to be effective in many environments, many project managers have been banished as self-directed teams have said, "We don't need you!"

We strongly disagree. There is certainly a place for an effective project manager on agile software development, infrastructure, process improvement, and change management teams. Agile teams need to ask, "What is the role of the Project Manager in this environment?" The impactful use of lean thinking for project management is for the project manager to take on the role of lean coach and value stream advocate.

When the term *agile project management*[26] is used, it typically implies the application of core lean (agile) concepts including:

- *Customer value focus*—As we're sure you've noticed, a central theme of lean is creating value for the customer and stakeholders. Agile project management stresses this concept and the supporting principle of *systemic thinking*: All activities that make up the stream of events that deliver a product or service[27] are interrelated and interdependent. You cannot change one element without impacting one or more of the other elements. Project managers who appreciate this insight play a key role on the team, ensuring that people *see the whole* and avoid local optimization at the expense of enterprise.

- *Emphasize the business problem*—Someone once said, "All IT projects are business projects or they should not be performed!" We endorse this sentiment and believe the key message is that it is the business problem/opportunity that informs the IT project and not the other way around. All too often, we see IT project proposals that are rich in technical benefits (e.g., a database upgrade,[28] more robust connectivity) that fail to identify and advocate for the business benefits the project will deliver.

- *Collaboration*—Shared learning is at the heart of any effective team. Very often, informative communication is an elusive objective. Anyone who has ever endured a project planning meeting or weekly status meeting can attest to this! Agile practices popularized daily standup meetings (also called Scrums or huddles) that have significantly increased collaborative discovery, commitment, and timely communication among team members and project stakeholders.

- *Value creation over task execution*—We've all been on projects where there was intense focus on task completion at the expense of value creation and emphasis was placed on *documented* precision, not actual reality.

    Agile project management is about acknowledging that the project plan is a static snapshot of our understanding of the problem or opportunity right now. The focus is on accuracy over the life of the project, not precision at any given point in time. We expect our understanding to change as we validate our speculation on how to proceed (see the section on Lean Startup and validated learning). Instead of mindlessly following a plan that we know is based on an incomplete understanding, we anticipate the plan will change as we learn more.

- *Plan–Do–Check–Act*—Building on the concept of learn-as-you-go, agile project management is applying the scientific method of learning to make course corrections grounded on fact-based discovery. This cycle is often referred to as PDCA.[29] Although this model is well known, it is deceptively simple and quite difficult to accomplish effectively. We'll explore PDCA thinking throughout this book.

- *Changing role of the project manager*—Lean project management extends agile project management practices beyond methods and tools and moves toward the realm of lean coaching. In a lean enterprise, project managers take on a more extensive role of coaching team members to apply new ways of behaving in order to learn for themselves how lean IT impacts the entire organization.

Lean IT Frontier

Since the release of the Agile Manifesto in 2001, the world of IT has seen a storm of innovation in how ideas are tested and validated, software is developed and released, teams are organized and led, and projects are managed. With the gains of agile, kanban, virtualization, cloud computing, Big Data, and Lean Startup, the time has come (at last) to explore how lean IT can transform IT as a key enabler of business results. These various disciplines of IT practice can be united to create a *unified field theory* with which to ignite an IT transformation! We will share examples of what has worked for others and for us, while providing a framework based on our lessons learned over 30 combined years of experience applying lean in IT, service, manufacturing, and healthcare environments.

Notes

1. John Naisbitt, *Megatrends: Ten New Directions Transforming Our Lives*, Grand Central Publishing, August 16, 1988.
2. Steven C. Bell and Michael A. Orzen, *Lean IT—Enabling and Sustaining Your Lean Transformation* (Boca Raton: CRC Press, 2011).
3. http://agilemanifesto.org.
4. Big Bang is the opposite of incremental, iterative change. It is letting all improvements and changes store up for a single release—much like activating every module of a new ERP system at go live!
5. More info on Scrum can be found at https://www.scrum.org/resources/what -is-scrum.
6. http://www.djaa.com.
7. We might be getting a little carried aware here to make a point. All shops have basic demand and capacity awareness, but the biggest gap seems to be the "yes we can" mentality as soon as there is some availability with no regard to the WIP in the system as a whole. So perhaps a requirements analyst is available, but the developers are maxed out. That can look like unused capacity so what we do is put that requirements analyst to work creating more WIP inventory!
8. Jez Humble and David Farley, *Continuous Delivery: Reliable Software Releases through Build, Test, and Deployment Automation*, Addison-Wesley, 2011.
9. Steve Blank, *Why the Lean Start Up Changes Everything*, Harvard Business Review, May 2013, p. 66.
10. See *The Four Steps to the Epiphany*, 2nd edition, by Steve Blank (K&S Ranch, 2013). This is the book that originally launched the Lean Startup movement.
11. See *The Lean Startup: How Today's Entrepreneurs Use Continuous Innovation to Create Radically Successful Businesses*, by Eric Reis (Crown Publishing, 2011). This book created a storm of interest and launched a worldwide movement extending Lean Startup concepts beyond high-tech companies to practically every type of business enterprise and organization (e.g., service, government, education, healthcare, manufacturing, travel, etc.).
12. http://lean-Startup.meetup.com.
13. http://itrevolution.com/manifesto/.
14. Gene Kim, Kevin Behr, and George Spafford, *The Phoenix Project: A Novel About IT, DevOps, and Helping Your Business Win*, IT Revolution Press, 2013.
15. http://itrevolution.com/the-three-ways-principles-underpinning-devops/.
16. James P. Womack and Daniel T. Jones, *Lean Thinking: Banish Waste and Create Wealth in Your Corporation–Second Edition*, Free Press, 2003.
17. Jeffrey Liker, *The Toyota Way: 14 Management Principles from the World's Greatest Manufacturer*, McGraw-Hill, 2004.
18. Steven C. Bell and Michael A. Orzen, *Lean IT—Enabling and Sustaining Your Lean Transformation*, Chapter 9 (Boca Raton, FL: CRC Press, 2011).
19. http://www.amazon.com/Best-Sellers-Books-Agile-Project-Management/zgbs /books/379406011.

20. http://www.pmi.org.
21. See Project Management Body of Knowledge (PMBOK) at http://search.pmi.org/?q=PMBOK.
22. http://www.scrumalliance.org/certifications.
23. http://blogs.collab.net/agile/qa-agile-certification-certified-scrummaster-or-pmi-agile-certified-practitioner-which-one-is-right-for-you#.UysD49wYq2N.
24. Even when the project has been performed in the past—say, deploying a virtual server—the universe has a way of changing the conditions so each deployment is not exactly the same!
25. Non-value-added work, also called NVA, refers to activities that do not create value for customers and stakeholders.
26. An in-depth look at Agile Project Management is available in Sanjiv Augustine's book, *Managing Agile Projects* (Prentice Hall, 2005).
27. This is also known as a Value Stream.
28. True story: a colleague of ours shared that his company had spent more than $600,000 on a database upgrade of a large enterprise system. When the project was 80% complete, it was discovered that the business had plans to move to a new platform!
29. PDCA is frequently referred to as the Deming Cycle, Shewart cycle, or PDSA (Plan–Do–Study–Act).

Chapter 2

The Transformation Framework

A bad system will beat a good person every time.

W. Edwards Deming

Introduction

To build an organization that will last, people must possess certain behavioral characteristics that are deeply embedded. It's useful to think of any transformation as having two key dimensions: technical and social. The technical side includes tools and methods, many of which have been adapted to the IT space.[1] In some ways, this part of the transformation is more accessible and inviting to organizations. People love tools, as they raise the promise of immediate action and commensurate results. Tools involve *doing* something that we usually equate with change for the better—often a faulty assumption based on emotions and hopeful aspirations. Technology is what we do; IT is especially vulnerable to looking to tools and technology as a silver bullet for organizational problems. Unfortunately, the typical positive impact of introducing a new tool is a temporary illusion at best. Tools have a place in a transformation, to be sure, but they do not normally change people's behaviors or thinking patterns!

The social side of a lean IT transformation is less tangible and quite illusive. Most of us know when we are working on a team with a dynamic culture of trust, transparency, professional challenge, and accomplishment where great results seem to come naturally, albeit with struggle. But very few people can actually explain why some cultures are so effective and others are absolutely toxic. "We need a new culture around here!" is a proclamation we hear often when working with organizations interested in adopting lean IT practices and the results they enable people to achieve.

The social side (people side) of a lean IT transformation is the behavioral and thinking piece of the puzzle. Companies have been trying to figure this one out for a very long time. In this chapter, we'll share a model framework we apply throughout this book—a *house* that shows the building blocks of a lasting transformation. Although the house metaphor is overused, we couldn't resist! Lean IT is all about building an effective IT organization, and the quality of the components used in building it make a huge impact on its stability and effectiveness. The house is a simple way to illustrate that lean IT is a system of many parts working together in unison.

The ideas in this book are based on years of trial and discovery of the sequenced steps to building a sustainable lean system. In other words, we have experienced many setbacks along the way that, upon reflection, check, adjust, and try again, have in some cases led to a better understanding of what really works. We still have much to learn but what we have discovered is reflected in the framework we are sharing with you. If you are a lean practitioner, you'll notice that many of the IT-based examples in this book can be effectively adapted to apply to all areas of your organization.

The Lean IT House

Let's take a look at the building blocks of our house (Figure 2.1).

Foundation

Perhaps the most common mistake we see is organizations attempting to make the leap from where they currently are to a more stable, capable, and productive workplace without first establishing a solid base from which positive change will flourish. In the foundation, key elements are identified that

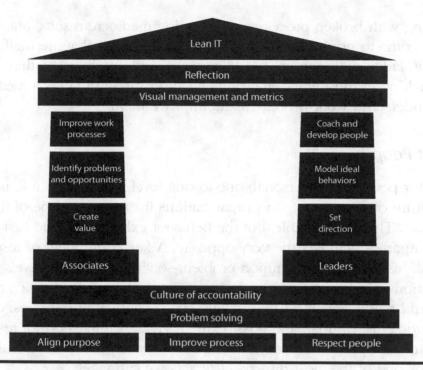

Figure 2.1 The lean IT house.

need to be in place in order to provide an environment in which enterprise excellence becomes a deep-seated organizational habit.

Align Purpose

The keystone of a solid transformation is a clearly defined, understood, and continually reinforced purpose. In many organizations, there is no shared definition or understanding of *why* the company exists. Mission statements become dusty, ignored plaques hanging on walls, and rarely translate into a shared aim throughout the business.[2] Purpose is frequently a loosely understood and individually applied underpinning of why we do the work we do. But when purpose is aligned, everyone in the organization can clearly answer the questions, "Why do we exist as an organization?" and "How does my work contribute to our goals?"

Improve Process

The work you do can and should be viewed as a process: Inputs are received, effort transforms something (product, service, information), and outcomes are passed on. We often see great people living by heroic efforts, contending with broken processes, and getting mediocre results. Many people have come to normalize and accept work processes that are ineffective, inefficient, laden with non-value-adding tasks, and utterly frustrating. What is clearly lacking in most work environments (and surely in IT) is a method to clearly understand work processes and improve them!

Respect People

Respect for people, at a personal, one-to-one level, plays a key role in building a culture of excellence. Most organizations list *respect* as one of their core values. This is admirable, but the behavior exhibited by the vast majority of companies is in fact the very opposite. A key component of respect for people[3] is developing common problem-solving skills at all levels of the organization—leaders, managers, and associates. Unseen leaders, command-and-control management decrees, vague goals, conflicting priorities, concealed problems, distrust, and gossip are all vivid examples of not respecting people! In our opinion, accommodating broken work processes as tolerable is perhaps one of the most disrespectful acts we can take!

Problem Solving

Most people will tell you problem solving is what they do all day: dealing with whatever issues come their way and doing whatever it takes to fix them. The problem here lies with autonomy, skill set, and overburden. People often don't have clarity of purpose and don't possess effective problem-solving skills or have enough slack time to notice obstacles until they become too large to easily solve. When they are that large, no one has time to solve them because they are overworked. It's a cruel cycle that is difficult to break.

An amazing insight is that, in practically every company we have visited, there is *no shared problem-solving method!* When people encounter a problem or improvement opportunity, they resort to a variety of methods including asking the boss, brainstorming, asking the 5 Whys,[4] starting an A3,[5] fishbone diagramming,[6] voting, selecting a similar problem from their past and repeating their response, or just plain guessing! When a shared routine of how we face, frame, understand, and address problems is present, the time to implement countermeasures and assess their impact is significantly reduced. At the end of the day, effective widespread problem solving drives organizational learning.

Culture of Accountability

We often hear people complain, "There's no accountability around here!" After spending years observing people doing their work and interacting with one another, we often see the same thing. So what fosters accountability? In organizations where personal responsibility and follow-through are common practice, we see a very distinct environment: one with significant differences in the areas of respect, trust, sense of common purpose, appreciation of process, standard work, shared problem solving, and visual management. It is these foundational elements which combine to support a culture of shared accountability.

The First Pillar: Associates—Where Value Is Created

The front line is where value[7] is created. In IT, we are talking about business analysts, developers, database analysts (DBAs), service desk techs, operations people, infrastructure architects, maintenance techs, and all other members of the delivery stream. Anyone who directly contributes to the development, implementation, operation, maintenance, and use of technology supports the flow of information, products, and services.

The first pillar consists of three behaviors that support a culture of excellence at the front line: create value, identify problems and opportunities, and improve work processes. Let's briefly look at them now and see how they are applied later on.

Behavior 1—Create Value

The essence of doing good work is the creation of value. The essence of doing the *right* work is the creation of customer value. When associates know what good work looks like, and work standards are aligned to customers' needs and expectations, great things happen.

When IT work is viewed with a product rather than a service mentality, an amazing shift occurs. Why? Because when you shift your perspective toward *delivering a product* rather than a service, customer value becomes the focal point. For product-focused organizations, it is clear what customer value is, because customers buy what they value and ignore what they don't! For service-focused areas of the business, customer value is not so evident and they are often characterized as a cost center. Here, the emphasis shifts to the pursuit of efficiency and cost control (often the stated goal of IT) while not giving much attention to deliberate value creation. This focus misses the whole point of lean and value creation.

In today's world, IT plays a central role developing, delivering, and supporting products that deliver value to customers. The key here is getting people in IT to understand the value they create. This can be challenging when IT staff are far removed from the customer—something you can remedy by having your staff spend more time with customer-facing end users or, better still, your end customers.

Behavior 2—Identify Problems and Opportunities

W. Edwards Deming said, "You can't improve what you do not measure." Measurements play a critical role in determining whether people are achieving targets. But unless we create an environment where identifying problems and opportunities is expected, safe, and welcomed, we will be relegated to a relentless cycle of reactive firefighting that typifies many IT shops. People need to know if they are winning or losing and if life is ever going to get better!

So much of the work that takes place in IT is undocumented, ad hoc, and performed in ways determined by the person performing the work, that it might be hard to envision standard work in all that complexity. When standard work is not the norm, everyone performs work according to *their* understanding of what needs to be accomplished and of how things should be done, resulting in high variability of quality and productivity.

The essence of standard work[8] is to move away from people doing work their way (based on individual opinion and experience) to everyone working in a more consistent fashion. When everyone on the team abides by the standard, we begin to intentionally impact variability. Standard work serves as a snapshot of what good work looks like and a baseline from which improvement can happen.

There is a common misperception that standard work hinders creativity. But the real purpose of standard work is to make repeatable work routines much more predictable and less burdensome, freeing time up for the creativity and thinking bandwidth essential for more challenging tasks. Standard work also introduces trust and discipline as common behaviors in any team. The term *discipline* often conjures up images of marching in single file or doing push-ups, but the discipline we're talking about is the shared agreement that team members will *honor the process*. It turns out that adhering to the current standard (until a better way is found) is a shared behavior found within all organizations that have successfully transformed their culture.

Behavior 3—Improve Work Processes (through Daily Kaizen)

Kaizen is a Japanese term meaning *Change for the Good* and is often used to describe continuous improvement activities. Most kaizen activity we see in the workplace is project based.[9] Projects are a great way to get started, to introduce tools and principles, and to carve out time for improvement, but there's a catch. The challenge with project-based kaizen is that it lacks the immediacy and emphasis of on-the-spot problem solving done in real time (as in right now). By their very nature, projects have a beginning, a middle, and an end. True kaizen does not have an end point and is continuous! The whole idea of continuous improvement is that it is *unceasing and without end*!

It is common that people learn lean methods and tools in a project-based setting (e.g., "Let's do an improvement project on Service Desk procedures!"). Although there is nothing inherently wrong with learning while working on a project, the transition from project-based work to daily improvement has many deep-seated barriers, both internal and external.

Our Project-Based Paradigm

Individually, we all view our work from a certain perspective. For example, if the majority of your work is reactive in nature (responding to emergencies and frequently switching tasks), then you are likely to view how good you are at doing your job by your ability to nimbly jump from issue to issue, quickly refocus, and take immediate action. Your personal paradigm toward work may not embrace the need for a deeper level of understanding cause-and-effect relationships or the value of developing countermeasures that go beyond attacking symptoms. Project-based improvement efforts reinforce this viewpoint because "there is simply no time to make improvement during my busy workday." After the kaizen project is *complete*, we go back to work and ostensibly suspend all improvement work!

The urgency and drama of the workplace often encourage reactive behavior, which places more importance on immediate action than it does on lasting results. If we can put out the fire today, we'll worry about tomorrow's problems when they come. And when we recognize and award heroic efforts and results at any cost, that is behavior we cultivate and encourage.

CADENCE

In order to get good at any new skill, practice is required. The more frequently we practice an activity, the more experience we gather and the more proficient we become. Cadence is the rhythm, pattern, and pace with which we practice. An established cadence creates predictability of activity for the team as well as for management and is a key ingredient in developing new habits.

Habits can be both a blessing and a curse. They reinforce behaviors that serve us well (working out at the gym) or they waste our time (aimlessly surfing the Internet). Some habits can be highly destructive, while others allow us to develop as human beings. The routine of an established cadence reinforces new behaviors until they are embedded deeply as habits. In *The Power of Habit*, Charles Duhigg points out that habits follow a general sequence: cue, routine, and reward.[10] A cadence implants a pattern, a pattern serves as a cue, a cue sparks a routine, and a reward reinforces the behavior. We'll explore the power of cadence throughout this book.

Improvement efforts that are exclusively project-based reinforce this reality and fortify reactive behavior.

Daily kaizen refers to the common practice of *stopping* when someone encounters a problem, *swarming* to see and understand, *thinking and acting* to deeply understand and improve, and *sharing* to broadcast the learning.[11] There is no boundary between doing work and improving work, so improvement is done continuously throughout the workday as problems and opportunities are encountered.

When frontline staff view their work in terms of value creation, actively look for problems and opportunities for improvement, and embrace an established cadence of daily problem solving, expectations become transparent and behaviors evolve to a new common norm. Over time, the shared actions, values, and beliefs of the team begin to change.

The Second Pillar: Leadership—Where Alignment Is Cultivated

Leaders—C-level executives, directors, and managers—either actively promote alignment of purpose through a value stream perspective or unwittingly encourage disorder among departments and functions. A value stream comprises all the people, activities, departments, and hand-offs necessary to create and deliver value to the customer (be it a product, service, or information). In IT, vertical silos often focus exclusively on their specific segments of the IT value stream to the detriment of the overall flow of value to the customer.

Frontline associates focus primarily on the *vertical* work in front of them and within their circle of control: their department, their team, and their piece of the work product. In order to generate improvement at the value-stream level, leadership is needed to coordinate efforts *horizontally* among various departments to achieve positive change that is experienced by end customers. Value stream management is much easier to describe than it is to successfully execute. When leaders move from managing functional silos to managing value streams, the inherent contradictions between the goals of each silo and the objectives of the organization become blatantly apparent!

It's not easy to shift from a localized focus of your functional area (e.g., infrastructure, security, project management). But effective leadership is more about supporting and coaching the development of people than about making proclamations and issuing orders. To do this well as a leader, you have to broaden your perspective.

Behavior 1—Set Direction

Strategy is about envisioning a future state and devising ways to reach it that will weather predictable as well as unforeseeable challenges. In a transformation, it is essential for leaders to position continuous process improvement as a central component of how to endure the obstacles that certainly lie ahead. A good strategy answers the question, "What are the most important things in this organization?" When *daily* continuous process improvement is absent from the strategic intent of leaders, a strong message is sent concerning the lack of priority and importance of embedding applied learning into daily work. People become conditioned to know when another program or initiative has arrived and learn that *this too shall pass*.

Newsflash: people think about and do what their boss talks about and does most often! Strategy can be intentional and deliberate or emergent and ad hoc. When strategy (and measurements) include key initiatives, budgets, project schedules, and operational performance, but fail to comprise targeted improvement of core business processes, few if any resources are allocated toward building a culture of enterprise excellence. It is the role of senior leadership, with the input of management, to articulate and reinforce a *shared* direction.

When strategy deployment[12] is measured and tracked, time and resources are allocated toward process improvement. This sends a clear message to people that the company is serious about continuous improvement and that it is here to stay. Be careful here: The goal is to create a culture of experimentation and alignment. This is *not* measured by number of kaizen events or inflated reports of improvement benefits.[13] See Chapter 10 for a discussion of strategy deployment.

Behavior 2—Model Ideal Behaviors

We've all heard the familiar phrase, *actions speak louder than words*. Leaders and managers communicate what is *really* important (and what is not) by the behaviors they demonstrate. It's great to talk about the importance of respect for people, continuous improvement, and commitment to operational excellence, but only consistent behavior will convince people that the transformation is real and here to stay!

People tend to model their actions based on values, beliefs, and work systems. Values and beliefs are unique, personal, and internally ingrained. We don't need to go there! Attempting to change someone's values is ill advised and probably futile. When *thought leaders* model actions and conversations we want prevalent in our workplace, people tend to gravitate toward new behaviors. Thought leaders are people of influence and not exclusively leaders and managers. In fact, the most influential thought leaders are often associates who consistently model ideal behavior while achieving great results.

When work systems are adjusted to drive ideal behaviors, culture begins to shift and a new normal begins to emerge. This takes years of relentless effort and learning: think 5 to 7 years or more. As you work through this field guide, you will be building the core work systems that influence behaviors to reinforce a culture of respect, engagement, and continuous improvement.

Behavior 3—Coach and Develop People

The development of people is perhaps the most essential factor in creating and sustaining a lean transformation and even more so in an IT environment. IT professionals often equate professional development with learning new technical skills such as mastering a new application or programming language. While this is a form of people development, the type of growth we are referring to here has more to do with problem solving, communicating, and effectively working within a team.

In order for people to learn new skills, they require training, the opportunity to practice, and a coach to support their progress. Of the lean transformations we have seen that under-deliver and stall out, 100% have included training, fewer have made adequate time to practice new skills, and *none* have done an adequate job of developing internal coaches to nurture people as they develop new ways of thinking and acting. Coaching is a learned skill but often we find inadequate training and support for internal coaches. One organization we worked with had a saying: "Everyone shall have a coach, and everyone will be a coach!" The intent of that edict was to make it clear that, without trained, capable coaches, the transformation was going nowhere.

Visual Management

A visual management system plays a key role in creating transparency in the workplace and aligning all levels of the organization. An effective visual management system clearly answers questions such as

- What are we currently working on?
- Are we completing our work on time?
- What is important today?
- What does success look like?
- Right now, are we winning or losing as a team?
- What are the challenges and struggles we are currently facing (quality, flow, delivery, safety, etc.)?
- What continuous improvement actions are in flight?
- What is the extent of problem solving in our team?

A visual management system ensures these questions are being asked and that the answers are understood at every level of the organization. The biggest impact of a visual management system is the promotion of meaningful communication between leaders, managers, associates, and departments. The outcome is an alignment of focus and behavior leading to great results from great behaviors. Much more on this topic can be found in Chapter 7.

Metrics

Imagine watching a sporting event without a scoreboard—pretty boring wouldn't you say? People need feedback to understand if the work they are doing is moving them toward a meaningful goal or not. Providing actionable feedback is spot-on respect for people. Meaningful, actionable metrics connect behavior with results and supply predictive indicators to make thoughtful course corrections. Without measurements, it isn't possible to assess performance or the impact of a change.

A central element of effective continuous process improvement is a common framework for problem solving. Perhaps the most accessible and widespread problem-solving method is the Plan–Do–Check–Adjust (PDCA)[14] problem-solving cycle. This structured approach to solving problems is at the same time easy to understand and deceptively difficult to execute. I cannot *check and adjust* if I do not know whether a change is in fact an improvement. Measurements and standards help in this regard.

Peter Drucker[15] said, "What gets measured gets managed." That's usually true, but perhaps an equally important point is, "Are we managing the right things?" Measurements drive behavior. If we measure things that are outside the direct control of the people being measured, we are wasting their time and disrespecting them. A feeling of helplessness can emerge as hope dims and disengagement becomes the team norm. As you will see, metrics and measuring the right things is more a process of discovery than it is an exact science.

Reflection

Careful evaluation of our work performance, our interactions, our potential growth, our actual progress, and ourselves as human beings is the final component of our house. The Japanese term used to describe this activity is *hansei*,[16] which relies on self-awareness and personal assessment as a process of self-improvement. Reflection requires courage to be honest about our weaknesses and humility to get comfortable with our blind spots and shortcomings. We can only improve those aspects of ourselves that we acknowledge need improvement!

The purpose of reflection is to honestly assess what characteristics of our behavior worked and what didn't work, and to act accordingly. This is similar to the Plan–Do–Check–Adjust cycle in that we must rigorously *check* our behavior, performance, and results to truthfully identify what needs to change. Like PDCA, on the surface this sounds very straightforward and simple. In practice, this is brutally difficult to accomplish!

Let's Get Started! Your Roadmap

A key factor of a successful journey is an effective map. A map helps keep you on course and safe when you might otherwise stray into uncharted and dangerous territory. To help you on your journey, we've created a roadmap for you to guide your path: this book! It will give concrete advice on how to get started building and sustaining your transformation. Like any map, it doesn't have all the answers. You'll hit roadblocks, detours, and also wonderful discoveries on the way. But, it will provide a starting point and a heading to come back to time and again to check whether you are making progress toward your destination.

The lean IT house highlights the concepts we'll explore as well as emphasizes the relevant building blocks you'll need. We hope that by giving you a conceptual map at the start, you'll have a mental model to lead a successful lean IT transformation. Let's begin!

Notes

1. See Chapter 1 for a discussion of the lean IT cosmos.
2. When we refer to levels in an organization, we denote three: (1) frontline workers (Associates), (2) people who are responsible for the performance of a group of people (Managers), and (3) those responsible for setting strategic direction and leading the organization (Leaders).
3. For a great read on this topic, see Freddy Ballé and Michael Ballé, *Lead with Respect* (Lean Enterprise Institute, 2014).
4. The 5 Whys is a lean problem-solving method of repeatedly asking "Why?" until the root cause of the problem is identified.
5. An A3 is a one-page form structured to reinforce Plan–Do–Check–Adjust thinking.
6. Fishbone diagramming is a cause-and-effect analysis method made popular by Kaoru Ishikawa in the 1960s.
7. Value is what customers expect to receive and are willing to pay for.
8. More on standard work and its uses can be found in Chapter 5.
9. Improvement projects are held over several sequential days or perhaps teams meet once a week over weeks or even months.
10. Charles Duhigg, *The Power of Habit* (New York: Random House, 2012), pp. 29–59.

11. This approach applies a small-scope PDCA, a problem-solving cycle of continuous improvement.
12. Strategy deployment, also known as hoshin kanri, is a structured approach to cascading vision, strategy, and measurable goals throughout the organization by focusing on shared goals throughout value streams, linking tactics to strategy, and measuring what matters (usually business fundamentals).
13. Don't mistake activity for results. This sort of *fake lean* is all too common.
14. PDCA forms the framework of lean problem solving. Based on the scientific methods, PDCA is an accessible and deceptively difficult way of thinking. See Mike Rother, *Toyota Kata* (McGraw–Hill, 2009), for perhaps the best exploration of PDCA as a problem-solving and a coaching routine.
15. Drucker was a management consultant and author whose work significantly contributed to the foundational principles of the modern business corporation.
16. *Hansei* means *critical reflection* and centers on acknowledging your mistakes and shortcomings in order to make a personal commitment to improve.

Chapter 3

The Importance of Purpose

Alice: Would you tell me, please, which way I ought to go from here?

The Cheshire Cat: That depends a good deal on where you want to get to.

Alice: I don't much care where.

The Cheshire Cat: Then it doesn't much matter which way you go.

Lewis Carroll
Alice's Adventures in Wonderland, 1865

Introduction

Now is a great time to discuss the ultimate reason to apply lean in your organization—something we refer to as True North (more commonly called *purpose*). Lean is the means by which we activate our commitment to continually improve, fulfilling our purpose as best we can, getting a little bit better at it every day. Surprisingly, purpose is rarely shared throughout all levels of a company. Common sense tells us that for the employees of an organization to perform at their best, they must understand the ultimate reason why the company exists. Knowing our purpose creates guideposts to direct both operational and strategic decision-making. While in many companies, management will post mission or vision statements on websites or plaster them on the walls of headquarters, seldom does it discuss these statements or use them to influence and direct the attention of associates. This is true regardless of the attributes of the company—small or large, for profit or nonprofit—a well-understood linkage between purpose, daily decisions, and behaviors is a rare occurrence.

In Chapter 4, *Day Zero*, you will find how to begin applying some basic practices to start your lean transformation in earnest. We'll show you simple ways to demonstrate immediate progress and grab the collective attention of your organization. By the end of Chapter 4, *Day Zero*, you will have informed the management team, provided basic training, communicated with frontline staff, and begun your visual management system and daily standups to drive accountability.

So what is the mechanism that ensures that all levels of your organization are focused on the right things—those issues and problems that are most directly aligned with the greatest needs of customers and objectives of the company?

In a word: purpose.

So what is purpose?

We like this definition: *The reason for which something is done or created or for which something exists.*

When people understand the *reason* something is done, they are provided the opportunity to understand, process, and internalize the activity. There is an old saying that goes, "People don't care about the what, until they understand the why." Shigeo Shingo[1] captured this idea when he said, "Know-how alone isn't enough! You need to Know-why! All too often, people visit other plants only to copy their tools and methods."

The purpose of an organization—its vision, goals, and objectives— plays a critical role influencing what work gets done and how it gets accomplished. Focusing on the right work is difficult because we tend to confuse activity with results. The mental focus and stress that come from being busy can distract us into assuming we are focused on the right things. The initial decision we all need to make is determining *what* work is the most important to do (problem facing). The next step is to view the problem within the correct context (problem framing). Only after we are focused on the right problem, and see it within the appropriate context, should we begin to solve it![2] It is very difficult to know where you want to go (and what kind of course corrections may be called for) if you do not have a destination in mind. Without a clear, measurable goal, teams and people are left with misaligned vague aspirations. The authors remember listening to Jim Womack[3] discuss the interrelation of *Purpose, Process, People.* To become a great organization, Womack posed three questions:

1. What is your *purpose?*
2. What *processes* achieve your purpose and how lean (effective) are they?
3. How do you engage your *people* to agree on purpose and create lean processes, with fulfilling work, to achieve the purpose?

Without a well-articulated purpose that is widely understood and accepted, people tend to create their own reasons for being at work. By their very nature, individually developed purposes are not shared, aligned, or inclusive. It is interesting to note that Womack starts and ends with purpose in these elegantly simple questions. It is purpose that provides the direction and insight needed for people to take responsibility to identify and solve those problems that matter most. Moving them from speculation to insight, we want staff to know, not to have to guess.

So what makes a good purpose statement? We've all seen company mission statements, vision statements, strategic plans, and declarations of purpose in annual financial statements. Sometimes we'll see a clear statement of purpose embedded within; often we do not. Let's take a look at a few good examples (some are extracts from more extensive pronouncements):

Zappos[4]: *To Live and Deliver WOW*
IBM[5]: *Dedication to every client's success. IBMers ...*
   – *Are passionate about building strong, long-lasting client relationships.*
   – *Are focused on outcomes. We sell products, services and solutions to help our clients succeed, however they measure success.*
   – *Demonstrate this personal dedication to every client.*
Mayo Clinic[6]: *To inspire hope and contribute to health and well-being by providing the best care to every patient through integrated clinical practice, education, and research.*
Oxfam[7]: *To create lasting solutions to poverty, hunger, and social injustice.*
Kiva[8]: *We are a non-profit organization with a mission to connect people through lending to alleviate poverty.*

It amazes us that, while lacking in specifics, well-stated purpose statements effectively provide the direction so that the staff can exercise judgment and take action appropriate to the situation. Show people the contribution of their daily work within the context of a meaningful purpose and they find a way to get there. Make your company's purpose—and how people fit in—crystal clear, and they will feel valued and actively find ways to move toward established targets and contribute in ways you didn't even think of.

What do you notice about these values/purpose statements? Here are a few elements to look for in a good purpose statement:

1. Clear, concise, and answers the question, *Why?*
2. Inspires and motivates people to act: build, focus, provide, create, connect
3. Memorable

Imagine your team living the organization's purpose with clarity and intentionality. What would that look like? What would be different about the way people interact? When writing a great purpose statement it is essential to think about what ideal behaviors you want to inspire and then filter that through the three preceding elements to create a purpose statement that motivates and inspires staff.

Now is a good time to take a look at your organization's purpose statement. You may refer to it as a vision or mission statement. Read it aloud as if you were reading it for the first time. Does it meet the preceding three criteria? Does it clearly and concisely answer the *why* question? Can the core elements be captured in a succinct sentence? Do you see people who are motivated to take action to openly address problems and are truly concerned about doing what is best for the customer, the company, and each other? Can you find evidence that your company's purpose is influencing and guiding daily behavior?

True North

True North is a great description of what an effective purpose statement provides: a clear sense of direction. The lean life is a life of aligned and intentional striving and continually taking small steps and making gradual progress toward a worthy goal. True North acts like a compass pointing in the correct direction and acts to describe how things should be, not only what we think we can do today. Just as the needle of a compass aligns with north, people align with your organization's purpose. This includes goals and aspirations around quality of your work, delivery performance, customer satisfaction, safety, productivity, people development, or any other worthy goal.

To better appreciate the impact of an effective purpose statement that provides a True North goal, consider the military, where the system of management is command-and-control, a highly directive system of supervision. In this type of a system it might seem as though the rank and file don't need to know the purpose of a mission or operation. But what happens if, during a battle, there is no commanding officer to issue orders? How do soldiers determine the best course of action to take? That's where *mission intent* comes in.

Mission intent provides a clear picture of the end-state by clearly calling out what results are expected. We find it interesting that, even in the military where people routinely follow the commands of their superiors, the importance of mission intent increases as the complexity and risk of the mission intensifies. How do you get staff to autonomously act in a way that is consistent with the purpose when they are under fire and can't find a supervisor? Mike's father, who enjoyed a career in the Air Force, liked to say, "Mission intent is essential when the bullets are flying because people need to make decisions based on the situation in front of them. They make informed decisions when they understand the objective of the undertaking."

In most organizations, and certainly in the world of IT, complexity is ever increasing, risk is a real issue, and the path to move from the current state toward an aspirational goal (see the purpose statements in the Introduction) is at best unclear and emergent. True North provides clarity around intention and purpose and positions people to make informed decisions that align to the reason for the company's existence. We often hear leaders lament, "How do I get my people to do the right thing without being told?" True North and the degree to which it is demonstrated in the behavior of your people in their everyday work is the right place to start your transformation.

True North for the IT Enterprise

A question we often get goes something like this, "Does the company need to have a single True North or can each functional area have its own?" By definition, everyone should be aligned to a single purpose, so the organization should have one True North statement. That said, we see great advantage in specific areas of the business actively interpreting the purpose statement to create a meaningful message and more definitive guidance for their team members. In IT, having specific goals around technology, security, user experience, data management, infrastructure, etc. provides clarity around the organization's information and communication technology strategic intent.

Think of it this way, "My organization's True North is to *change the world through courageous discovery and innovation.* How does IT contribute to our shared aspiration?" The unifying impact of True North is that it is impossible to be successful in one area of the business if we don't succeed as a whole in moving toward our purpose. Each department, functional area, team, and individual strives to be a positive factor gradually moving toward True North.

Don't overdo it though; it is easy to go down the path of having too many True North statements. Go to great pains to make sure that individual department purpose is aligned like a laser to the purpose of the company. Nothing will slow down strategy faster than each department acting as its own separate entity. As Dr. Stephen R. Covey said, "The main thing is to keep the main thing the main thing."[9]

Alignment—Using Purpose as a Plumb Line

When carpenters needs to build a cabinet so that it is aligned and squared to the window next to it, they uses a plumb line as a reference tool. A plumb line is a string with a weight suspended at its end, as shown in Figure 3.1. Gravity pulls the string straight toward the ground to create a vertical reference line. Purpose acts in the same way because the organization's reason for being acts much like gravity, orienting and pulling everyone (hopefully inspiring them) toward a common direction and a higher purpose.

Figure 3.1   A plumb line.

Why is it so important to gain clarity of purpose among everyone in your team, department, and company? The reason has everything do to with alignment. Most organizations have capable people who come to work to do a good job, but are mired in broken processes, uncoordinated handoffs with other departments and people, and conflicting priorities. People need to understand and identify with their organization's intention to begin to understand how their personal goals line up.

As you mobilize your lean IT transformation by applying the systems in this book, you'll begin to galvanize purpose within your people. A common True North is superior as it provides an organizational plumb line. If you don't have a unifying company vision to rally around, purpose can be framed around team or department goals, but eventually you'll need to move toward a shared organizational purpose. It is a process that takes years to fine-tune. As you start out, focus on clarifying a purpose that really matters and resonates with your team.

Alignment has a lot to do with understanding purpose within the context of your specific environment and the challenges you are currently facing. Because the path to get to the next level of performance is never clearly marked, we need a means to illuminate and clarify the way.

Once there is clarity around purpose (why are we here?) and values (what is most important to us?), it is not difficult for people to begin to see how their personal goals align with team goals, which align with departmental goals, which align with company goals. When everyone can answer the question "How does my work support the goals of the company?" alignment begins to take root. We like to refer to this as *line of sight*: when everyone has clear vision connecting personal purpose with the purpose of the organization.

Begin your transformation now. You don't have to wait until everyone in your company is on the same page regarding your reason for being. But never lose sight of this goal. In our experience, enterprise alignment is *the* major element of enterprise excellence that gets plenty of lip service and very little constructive attention. Perhaps it is because purpose is so seldom defined in terms that are easily deciphered into action that we lack a meaningful goal to rally around. If your purpose is to deliver IT services with excellence and value, visualize what that specifically means in terms of daily work—for example, *We all know priorities, Nothing unclear,* and *All fields labeled*—and then begin to recognize obstacles and develop experiments to try to improve using structured problem solving.

Practice at Defining Purpose

Before finishing this chapter, let's start preparations for your Day Zero kick-off and develop a purpose statement. If your company already has one in place, we recommend you still work through this exercise and then compare your work with the published version to assess its effectiveness.

Begin by asking your team a few questions and jotting down some ideas:

1. What is the most important thing our company does?
2. Who do we serve with our products and services?
3. How are people (customers, employees, suppliers, community) impacted by the work we do?
4. How is the world different because of the contribution we make?

Now revisit a few examples of effective purpose statements:

Zappos: *To Live and Deliver WOW.*
IBM: *Dedication to every client's success.*
Oxfam: *To create lasting solutions to poverty, hunger, and social injustice.*

Next, recall the characteristics of a good purpose statement:

1. Clear, concise, and clearly answers the question, *Why?*
2. Inspires and motivates people to act: build, focus, provide, create, connect
3. Memorable

It is the role of leadership to provide an actionable purpose that resonates with your people. It is likely your company already has a mission, vision, values, or purpose statement, so use this exercise to assess its effectiveness. If you don't have a formal purpose statement (or your current one has become corporate wallpaper and lost its meaning), consider developing a new purpose statement:[10]

1. Apply the preceding three characteristics of a good purpose statement to create two or three versions (more if you'd like) of your purpose statement.
2. Using a colored pen, underline the phrases you like in each variation.
3. Take the underlined sections and blend the best of each to form a single purpose statement.

4. Read the new statement and ask yourself if it meets each of the three characteristics of a good purpose statement as outlined above. If the answer is *no* for any of the three, make revisions to your purpose statement to address that specific characteristic.

5. Once you are satisfied that the major characteristics of a good purpose statement have been addressed, socialize it to get feedback on its effectiveness and make adjustments as required:

   a. Include leaders, managers, and associates to get a good representation of opinion.

   b. Have them read the purpose statement and ask them the following questions:

      i. "Based *only* on what you read, what is the most important thing we are here to accomplish?"

      ii. "Why are we here working together?"

      iii. "Are you motivated when you read this statement? Why/why not? If so, toward what?"

      iv. "What would happen if we had a shared understanding of these goals?"

   c. Be sure to takes notes during these conversations (or ask if you can record them) because you'll often hear some great ideas and phrases you may want to use.

   d. Repeat the process until you are satisfied with your purpose statement.

You may be surprised at how effective this exercise is at revealing the impact of your current purpose statement. If people cannot demonstrate how it enables them to answer the four questions in statement 5(b), it may very well be time to revisit your company's purpose and the way you are conveying it!

Note: A purpose statement can be developed for an organization, division, region, department, or team. The key is to ensure alignment of everyone's purpose by using the organization's purpose statement as a plumb line (see "Alignment—Using Purpose as a Plumb Line").

Direction

Regardless of whether your company has a published mission, purpose, or True North statement, it is essential that you have agreement on a clearly articulated purpose among leaders, managers, and team members who will be working with you on the lean transformation. Involving people in the development and updating of your purpose statement will generate buy-in and support. If you are not certain that clarity, understanding, and consensus[11] are in place, go back to leadership and spend more time with them. You'll be glad you did. Without a clear direction, your transformation is at risk of being tasked with forging a new trail forward without a map and compass. The map is the course that will emerge as you experiment and learn from experience. The compass must first be in place!

Notes

1. Dr. Shingo was a consultant who worked with Taichi Ohno in the development of the Toyota Production System. He was considered the world's leading expert on manufacturing practices and the Toyota Production System. http://en.wikipedia.org/wiki/Shigeo_Shingo, last modified July 14, 2015.
2. Thanks to Michael Ballé for his ideas on problem facing and framing.
3. Jim Womack, "The Power of Purpose, Process, People" webinar, Lean Enterprise. http://www.lean.org/, May 1, 2008.
4. https://s3.amazonaws.com/zidownloads/TheZapposFamilyCoreValues.pdf.
5. http://www.ibm.com/ibm/values/us/ (only partially listed here—*shared values in action*).
6. http://mayoclinichealthsystem.org/locations/eau-claire/about-us/mission-vision-and-value-statements.
7. http://www.oxfam.org/en/our-purpose-and-beliefs.
8. http://www.kiva.org/about.
9. Kevin Kruse and Stephen Covey, 10 Quotes That Can Change Your Life, Forbes Magazine, July 16, 2012. Available at http://www.forbes.com/sites/kevinkruse/2012/07/16/the-7-habits/.
10. This could be accomplished by the leadership team or assigned to a subgroup using cross-functional focus groups to check its effectiveness.
11. Consensus as we use it here means, "I agree to support the decision of the group's majority." You do not need unanimous support to move forward.

Chapter 4

Day Zero

You will travel in a land of marvels.

Jules Verne

Introduction

Perhaps the most difficult step to take in a lean IT transformation is the very first. We've seen many companies with the best of intentions start talking about lean—they send staff to conferences, go on gemba[1] walks, and become quite excited about their coming transformation, only to fizzle and never really get started. Why? A big reason why companies fail on their journeys is that they do not know how to take those first formative steps to ensure a solid start. They get lost trying to figure out where to start—asking questions such as, "What processes, practices, and tools should be used to build a solid foundation for the transformation? Not wanting to make a mistake from the beginning, they never get started in the first place. And while those first steps do not need to be (and in fact will not be!) perfect, they are critical in building credibility and visibility for the transformation. Visibility is essential to keep the interest of the decision makers in the organization and get everyone's ongoing attention. So much of a transformation's longevity is dependent on gaining the collective attention of the executive team, introducing a story that captures their imagination and keeps them wanting for more. Perfection is the enemy at this point; you need a start that is good enough to begin to build your lean organization.

At the end of Chapter 3, your homework was to determine the purpose of your transformation—your True North, the compass setting that will guide the direction and course corrections along your path. In this chapter you will take the first steps on that journey that will move the lean transformation from theory to action. These are steps the authors have taken in leading companies on their journeys and steps we have observed in companies effectively implementing lean IT. Along the way we'll take a look at some of these companies, both successes and failures, as examples to learn from. Ultimately, you must decide which steps to take, but we will be with you each step of the way. Commit to taking concrete action sooner rather than later—let's get started and get that ever-difficult first step out of the way. It's important to get into the habit of applying PDCA (Plan–Do–Check–Adjust) thinking directly to the transformation, treating every step as an experiment to constantly test understanding, observe the results, and adapt based on the evidence.

Before applying any lean thinking or tools, first decide where to start in the organization. This choice is important and should not be made in haste. You need to select a *model line*,[2] an area where you can apply the principles and tools, learn, make adjustments, demonstrate success, and then apply what has been learned to other areas. This model line serves as both a proving ground and an ongoing laboratory that will be used in rousing support within the organization.

You are looking for a few things when choosing the model line:

1. An organization, function, or department complex enough to be credible when talking about results, but not so complex as to prohibit a reasonable chance of success. Size is also a factor; our recommendation is to start with a group of 100 people or less in large IT organizations; smaller organizations should get started with a group of perhaps 10–20 people
2. Enthusiastic support—or at least a general interest and no public opposition or hostility[3]—from the local management team
3. Sufficient time, interest, and resources available from management and frontline associates (requirements will be described later)
4. A willingness to learn and apply new ways of acting and thinking, and being comfortable with the uncertainty that goes with discovering innovative ways of doing work and improving work processes

CASE STUDY: NO SUPPORT FROM THE TOP

A Fortune 500 healthcare company with success in applying lean in multiple functions decided to undertake a similar journey in IT. The transformation was championed by a few middle managers with a vision for the future. On the surface these managers did everything right—they used the experience the company already had in other departments as a foundation, they built a great business case to show how the changes would positively impact the business, and they drew inspiration from the lean community by going on gemba walks and collaborating with other companies that had walked the same path. One thing they did not do was to gain executive support at the highest levels in IT.

The team made progress in the beginning and had some quick wins. But when it came time to make some tough decisions and change the fundamental way work was done, the bottom fell out. The transformation crumbled without an executive to stand up and provide necessary air cover for the team to continue their work. The team could not get approval to dismantle the old command-and-control approach to IT nor were they allowed to make any changes to the software development process. In the end, without executive support to sustain the gains, even the small wins achieved reverted back to the old, less effective way of doing things. The entire experience was particularly demoralizing to the team and other areas of IT that had been watching to see how things would turn out.

Spend some quality time applying these four guidelines to select the right place to start. Measure twice, cut once—you often only get one opportunity to make a first impression and convince people the transformation can really work.

Now that you have identified and recruited a group or function that will be the model line, it is time to solidify the support and operational models. If this is your organization, it certainly simplifies things, but let us assume that you are neither the CIO nor an IT director within the group, but rather outside the direct leadership reporting structure for the organization. The first order of business is to gain executive sponsorship within the group. Get an executive sponsor at a level as high as possible in the direct management chain of the organization who is inclined and able to provide active support—including time commitment and the willingness to participate in the transformation.

CHOOSING AN EXECUTIVE SPONSOR

✓ Willing to commit 2–4 hours per week
✓ Influencer in the company
✓ Willing to alter his or her own way of working
✓ A natural *learner,* not a *knower*
✓ Leads with humility
✓ Experienced in change management
☒ Always the one talking
☒ Not willing to make a firm time commitment
☒ Not respected in the company
☒ More interested in getting ahead than improving
☒ Uncomfortable not having all the answers

Ideally, this sponsorship would come from the top—the CIO or even the CEO, but often this is not possible.[4] The main objective is to demonstrate success and capture the attention and encouragement of the senior executive team.

Your executive sponsor provides vocal and demonstrable support for the transformation; in fact, executive sponsors will be going through a transformation of their own during the process. As you'll learn throughout this book, the transformation of IT teams is heavily dependent on the transformation not only of the frontline associates, but also of the management teams. We will focus not just on the way management teams view and interact with their teams as they go through the transformation process, but also on the roles and responsibilities of management in the new organization. In fact, the local and executive managers for the model line *must lead* the transformation. You may be in charge of the transformation or a subject matter expert in lean, but to gain buy-in of the associates and managers, it's critical that the direct management team is leading the work. This will require all the influential and political skills you possess!

Practice Makes Perfect

Our philosophy in executing the transformation has a bias for action and learning while doing. We've found that behavior-driven lean transformations have a much greater chance of success than heavy classroom style training. This is not to say that you won't do any classroom work or reading, but those learning methods supplement the learning that occurs at the gemba. The best way to think about this is that it is easier for the organization and staff to *act their way into thinking* than to think their way into acting.[5] How often have you seen training programs that get people excited about a new way of working or learning a new skill only to lose the knowledge before getting a chance to put it into action? We have seen countless companies send staff to classes such as Certified ScrumMaster[6] training and believe when they come back they'll lead the organization through an agile transformation. Most are left disappointed with the results. The amount of information provided in a classroom, without an opportunity to start using the learning, is simply too much to retain. You must create an environment that provides the information needed and quickly get people using that knowledge to ensure it sticks. Learning about lean and implementing lean are not the same thing!

Change management is often addressed in a clinical fashion—it's a distinct effort that runs parallel to the process changes, often by a consultant or other dedicated resource. Many large companies have hired outside consulting firms or created entire competencies around change management. Your lean transformation will certainly benefit from an understanding of the mechanics behind why people do or do not change their actions and thinking, but we suggest making it easy on yourself—spare the expense of the consultant and focus on learning by doing and getting people into the habit of applying lean.

From this point forward, think about the transformation from two viewpoints: management and frontline associates. Their perspectives are different and you must account for this in effecting the transformation. Managers have a broad view of the business needs and vision of where the company needs to go; frontline associates have the know-how to execute and improve the daily processes that make that vision a reality. We will share with you an approach to employ for each group and how to bring the groups together to create a foundation for your lean system.

Management's First Steps

First things first—the management team of the group going through the initial transformation needs enough information to get started, but not so much that it becomes overwhelmed. Let's take a look at how to inform and educate them about this coming change.

We've often found that middle management is by far the trickiest part of the lean transformation and also has a disproportionate amount of influence on the ultimate success of the effort. This group of people often perceive that they have the most to lose from the change of becoming a lean organization. The idea of an empowered workforce, where it's no longer the manager's job to solve all the problems and direct others on what to do, can be a frightening prospect for some managers (and exhilarating for others!). Through the transformation they'll come to understand that lean actually gives them more responsibility and greater impact on company strategy and results, but that will not be readily apparent at first.

There's a balance between providing enough information for context and our bias for action. We have to create an environment that makes people feel comfortable with (or at least not threatened by) change while not arming those that will use the information to try to battle the transformation team. To do this, we suggest the following principles for the management transformation:

1. Do not overload the management team with details they do not need (until they need them). For instance, there's no need to go into the details of strategic deployment or other advanced lean concepts the first time you introduce the foundational ideas of lean!
2. Focus on connecting the work of managers to the value-adding processes of the front line. Make the transformation about providing ever-greater value to customers, not a *management efficiency* program.
3. Address any negativity or sabotaging of the transformation with speed and directness. While almost without exception the developers, testers, analysts, DBAs, and other frontline IT staff will be able to make the leap to lean, some managers simply will not. This is critical: One influential manager actively working against the transformation can kill it! When that happens, move quickly to work with the person and, if required, find alternative work in another area—outside the company if necessary.

DAY ZERO STEPS TO TAKE WITH MANAGEMENT
1. Inform the management team
2. Provide basic lean education
3. Communicate to frontline staff
4. Implement visual management
5. Implement standups
6. Provide ongoing education and coaching

Management teams rightfully do not like to be surprised about major transformations, or any change for that matter. The first step is informing them of the effort, ideally in person. No one likes to hear through e-mail that his or her world is changing. And please refrain from using social media for this first announcement. Twitter is not the best medium for change management at this point in time!

At the initial meeting the executive sponsor should be prepared to discuss the framework for the transformation, what is expected of the management team, and when they will receive more information. It's not necessary to have everything figured out, but you should be able to clearly describe the *why* and talk about the approach that will be used.

After the first meeting, the model line management team needs some basic education on the topic of lean—what it is and what it is not. Many managers have an outdated view of lean—namely, that it is only about waste elimination or is code for firing people. This training should introduce lean IT as a systemic approach to operating and leading the group. It should not be geared to give the management team a doctorate in lean; anything more than a day or two[7] of information at this point is overkill. We want everyone to use a common language and get comfortable with the purpose of the journey that he or she is embarking on.

This is also a great time to take some gemba trips to see lean in action. If you are fortunate enough to have contacts at great lean companies, ask if you can bring your management team on a field trip to see what lean in action looks and feels like. Visit companies that demonstrate great lean thinking; don't worry about whether they are IT examples. Often the best learning comes from seeing lean outside the context of technology. Go on a gemba walk in a hospital or manufacturer, for instance, and discuss with your team what they saw and how it applies to your company. One caution is to set appropriate context with the participants; it's easy in the early days to think you'll never be as good as the companies you visit and use that as an excuse not to start in the first place. Going from the perspective of a traditionally managed company to see a mature lean organization can be a bit of a culture shock and leave visitors feeling as if lean is an unattainable aspiration. But with the right context, most management teams are energized by what they see and come away with a determination to make this their new reality. Gemba visits are an important part of your journey; have an end in mind before you head out. What are you hoping to see, learn, and achieve from the visit?

Now that the management team has some basic knowledge, it's time to get them moving and have some fun. Two lean tools to focus on right away for both management and front line associates are visual management and daily standup meetings. We use these as a starting point for transformation due to their relative ease of implementation and high payback. This is precisely what is needed to gain interest from those around you to enable the team to undertake more advanced and hard-to-observe practices that will form the foundation of your lean system. We will go into much more detail about these and other lean systems as well as the principles that guide us in choosing to start with them, but for now we'll provide enough information to get you started.

Before jumping into standups and visual management, this is also the right time for your sponsor to communicate (preferably in person) to the whole organization. The purpose of this first contact is to outline why the company or department is undergoing a lean transformation as well as what to expect and, very importantly, what is expected of everyone. The first communication sets the tone and context for the entire process and kicks off the transformation in earnest. While the most effective communication style depends upon company culture, in general the message should be upbeat and focus on increasing value to all stakeholders—including associates.

Visual Management and Standups

Two critical concepts to any lean transformation are visuality (Chapter 7) and accountability (Chapter 9). Visuality plays the critical role of ensuring that everyone has the right information when and where that information is needed; accountability is the mechanism to ensure that what is supposed to happen does happen and that process improvement stays in focus. There is no one right way to begin a transformation, but our experience has shown that these simple practices are an effective place to start. Others might choose value stream mapping or kaizen training, but nothing seems to grab an organization's attention more than seeing visible, quick evidence of the day's issues and progress being made. Let's take a look at how these two lean tools apply to the management team.

Visual Management System

To start building your new visual system for the management team, choose a location that is visible to the workforce, not hidden away in an office or locked conference room. This will be the site of your visual management system as well as the location of your standup meetings. Location is important in creating an environment of transparency. As the transformation proceeds, your culture will shift to one of openness, honesty, and responsibility, and you need to start demonstrating those principles from day one. There is no better way to demonstrate transparency than by making the management team visuals available for anyone in the organization to study. Make sure there is plenty of space for the visuals at the location you choose. We prefer magnetic whiteboards directly on the walls to allow for both writing directly on the boards and hanging visuals, but bulletin, cork, and other surface boards work as well. If the walls are unsuitable for this purpose, purchase rolling boards or kiosks. Don't let your physical workspace be a roadblock to getting started.

Your first visual management board needs only a few sections (listed here), but feel free to add others based on your needs. This board will evolve as the transformation progresses:

1. True North and the performance metrics that support it (preferably leading indicators, but more on that later) including posted simple definitions of red/green status
2. A management work-in-progress (WIP) board—representing the assignments of managers related to process improvements and the lean transformation
3. The status of your *production floor*—representing the value-added work of the model line, including any escalated problems or issues

Create boards that are easy to use and simple to understand. A quick test that can determine if you have succeeded is the *5 feet, 3 seconds rule*.[8] If you cannot easily see your board and in a matter of a few seconds determine what issues need attention, keep working on the design. Use clear visual controls and definitions with posted *rules* of use.

Your production floor measures will vary based on the type of work the organization does—they may be project status, number of incidents in progress, server builds, research projects in process, or a myriad of other things. The principle is to represent the value-added work in flight. These measures are a roll-up of the frontline visual system that you will also create (covered later in this chapter). It is important that the management and frontline boards are linked, ensuring that what is important to the organization is represented on each. The difference between the frontline and management visuals representing the production floor is in the level of granularity displayed.

Involve the whole management team in the design of the boards, using examples from your own experience, adapted from gemba visits, or downloaded from our site. Don't overengineer the boards—only put up what you are able to sustain. The only thing worse than no visual management is visual management that is not kept up to date. Stale visuals become a running joke in the organization and a reminder of the latest failed improvement program.

While you should expect your board to morph quite a bit in the near future, setting up a simple system such as this allows you to get the management team in the habit of using lean thinking—making things visible, creating accountability, and focusing on process improvement. Don't worry—you'll have plenty of time to make improvements.

Standup Meetings

Once you have a visual system established for the management team, standup meetings that occur at these boards should start. You may be familiar with the basics of standups due to their extensive use in agile; we will tweak things just a bit to get the most value for the management team.

You may be wondering why we are suggesting standups for a management team. The objectives of standups for management are very similar to why we implement them for frontline teams: namely, driving accountability, increasing collaboration, focusing on process improvement, and problem solving. The need for standups is perhaps more profound for management, where the work is often completely hidden and sometimes viewed with suspicion by frontline associates. Combining standups with visual management allows daily focus on the value-added work of managers—coaching, problem solving, connecting with associates and their work.

Those of you with exposure to agile teams are very familiar with the traditional three questions answered by each team member at standup: "What did I do yesterday?" "What am I going to do today?" and "What are my blockers?" These questions quickly focus the team with the intent of getting everyone up to speed very quickly (15 minutes or less) and setting the stage for collaboration and any additional conversations that need to happen after the standup.

The management standup is similar, but with some nuances. In Chapter 9, we'll talk about a tiered management system that will link different layers of standup meetings, but for now this will be your blueprint. Unlike our frontline teams, this first incarnation of the management boards does not need a standup meeting every day. We've found that this is a commitment that very

CASE STUDY: NO COPYING ALLOWED

We worked with a company that had built a visual management system around something they saw during a gemba visit to a Shingo Prize Winner.[9] An entire wall of the company cafeteria had been converted to an elaborate collection of strategy charts, Six Sigma project posters, lean project A3s,[10] safety information, and corporate vision and mission posters. The display was quite impressive and certainly gave the appearance of a company dedicated to lean thinking and process improvement. But when we spoke with staff throughout the visit, they had no idea of the purpose of the wall and never used it in the course of their daily work. To them it was just elaborate wallpaper with limited meaning and no direct influence on what they did every day.

A key idea of lean thinking is to *adapt* tools and methods you see and read about to your specific environment and challenges. Unless your team puts its own interpretations into the application of lean methods and tools, it simply will not become embedded and will quickly fade away. Putting up pretty visuals without connecting them to the daily work is not lean thinking. Don't copy what you see somewhere and expect that, by just creating a visual system, you have created a lean organization. Visual management is one aspect of a lean system and does not provide much value without supporting processes and people engagement.

few managers will make on day one. If you can get them to agree to meet two or three times per week, you're ahead of the curve at this point.

The format of the standups is simple: 15 minutes or less, with participation by everyone on the management team. Unlike agile team standups, which advocate team ownership, we recommend the senior leader of the group facilitate the standup. This will help as we evolve the boards to incorporate further accountability processes in Chapter 9. The standup should focus on all three parts of the board: status of performance metrics, status of the production floor, and the work in progress.

Some Do's and Don'ts for Management Standups

- DO review the status of the production floor every standup
- DO focus on escalated problems, risks, and issues
- DO assign new WIP process improvements with clear responsibility

- DO discuss progress of existing WIP
- DON'T review or add things already baked into your operations (such as year-end performance reviews)
- DON'T solve problems in the standup
- DON'T hide information—if it is important it should be on the board

In the standups, focus on value-added management activities and the transition to lean management. Examples of activities to add include coaching needed in the organization, improvement of management processes, key work systems that require development, and opportunities to better link tactical work to company strategy.

True North metrics may not need to be reviewed at every standup, as strategy and mission are not as volatile as daily problems and metrics tied to delivery work. Do implement a regular cadence for review of these metrics, perhaps every 2 weeks or once a month; experiment to see what works best for your organization. Key to success is creating a repeatable and predictable pattern for your management standup meetings, which will become an indispensible tool for leading the organization.

Implementing management standup meetings and visual management is a great first step on the organization's lean journey. These two practices create a solid foundation that will ensure that the organization doesn't lose interest in the transformation and leaders in the organization are focused on the things needed to drive positive change and ensure success.

Frontline Associates' First Steps

The journey for your frontline associates begins with the announcement from the executive sponsor as described earlier. It contains the critical

---

DAY ZERO STEPS TO TAKE WITH FRONTLINE ASSOCIATES
1. Communication from senior management explaining the lean transformation
2. Conversation with manager
3. Access to further information and learning
4. Implementation of visual management
5. Implement standups

---

information the associates need to make sense of the coming changes. The announcement should be followed very quickly by a conversation between each associate and his or her direct manager that is focused on reassurances about the intent of the transformation. This dialogue is critical; you should equip the management team with talking points to handle the concerns and questions that are bound to come up: "What does this mean to me?" "Is my job safe?" "Things are pretty good; why are we doing this?" and from the optimists in the group, "How do I get involved?" If the transformation is aligned to your True North, you should have no trouble responding to these questions. If it is not, before going forward you need to think deeply about how the transformation can be positioned to support your True North and how it will benefit the company's associates.

While you will implement similar systems and tools to what was put in place for the management team, the approach for the associates will diverge somewhat. The focus will be directly on the activities we want associates to start practicing. Unlike the management team, there's no need at this point to provide generalized lean training.[11] Learning will occur as you deploy the practices in the workgroups. For instance, talking about why we do standup meetings can occur as you practice the first standup. All change is messy, but active coaching and learning while doing makes it more understandable and easier for everyone.

At the same time, some people will want more information, and you should help them to learn the way that's best for them. Provide them resources to learn more on their own or in small groups. You can do this by starting a small lean lending library, leading or encouraging others to begin a book study club, or setting up gemba walks to see lean in action. Pay attention to the people that get involved; they are your future change agents—the first adopters and potential evangelists.

Getting Started

A traditional approach to transforming the front line involves using a value stream mapping exercise to understand current state and find the sources of waste. A value stream map (VSM) is used rather than process maps in order to illustrate that any one group or process is part of a bigger ecosystem. Value stream mapping helps to avoid optimizing the parts at the expense of the whole. While we can't argue with the logic of this approach, we have too often seen VSMs become nothing more than academic exercises. An external or internal lean consultant working with staff and management subject matter experts creates the map and identifies a myriad of potential improvements, most of which are never attempted. The exercise becomes one of so many paper exercises that never result in real, sustainable change.

Please don't misinterpret our message—we believe value stream mapping is a very important tool in a lean IT transformation that you should make use of, but we are going to start with small steps and build from there.

Visual Management System

Just like the management team, our first lean system to implement with the front line is visual management. This will create some buzz for the model line as well as draw your executive sponsor and management team into the space, allowing them to see tangible signs of change in the organization. It will also create a connection immediately between the management and frontline lean system. Your first visuals for the associates serve to build a foundation for more advanced tools and principles later: namely, accountability and a team-based problem solving culture.

Similarly to what we discussed for the management boards, choose a location that is easily accessible and visible to the associates. These boards will be used every day and the associates need access on a constant basis— find the best location and don't hide it away somewhere. Later chapters will cover collaborative spaces and the benefits offered in that type of a workspace. Don't worry if that's not your current situation. It doesn't pay to wait for the perfect facilities layout;[12] even if everyone is in cubes, put up the visuals where you can.

Effective visual management systems answer a few key questions: As a team, are we winning or losing? What are the most important things to work on? What issues require attention (these can be problems or opportunities for improvement)? To start to address these questions, begin with two concepts on the visual boards at this point: work in progress and problems.

Work-in-Progress (WIP)

A WIP board is essential for a few reasons in order to show:

1. The total work to be completed
2. Prioritization of the work
3. Where bottlenecks are occurring

A common problem in IT (and everywhere else for that matter), regardless of the specialty, is more demand than capacity. Unfortunately, lean cannot instantly solve that problem![13] There's likely always going to be more work to be done than the team can possibly accomplish. Where lean can help, though, is by making sure the amount of demand is visible and ensuring that the work that does get done is of the highest value to customers and is done in the most efficient manner possible. To start down that path, create a WIP board for your model line. Depending on the number of teams in scope for your transformation, this may be one board or it may be many.

The simplest versions of these types of boards have three columns: To Do, Doing, Done. A note card with a needed task or activity is placed in the appropriate column. Let's expand the card information just a little and add a few additional features: specifically, the expected completion date and the status of the task or activity—either on track or not, red or green.[14] Additionally, let's create another column and series of rows on the board to show who is assigned ownership of the card. All work for the team should be represented on the cards. If the team performs a task or activity, it should be represented on the board. This allows the visual system to accurately represent the full scope of work and enables a view of work flow for both value-added and non-value-added work items. A simple example can be seen in Figure 4.1. Spend some time and create WIP boards for each of the teams that are in scope for your transformation.

Be sure that you involve the frontline practitioners in the creation of the boards and tracking cards. Nothing will stall progress as fast as a staff that feel like change is being done to them, rather than with their input.

Problems

Problem solving is *the* most critical skill for people in a lean organization. We will always have problems. Let's say that again—we will always have problems. If anyone tries to tell you that an improvement system will make problems obsolete and a thing of the past, run the other way. If you can't find a problem in your operations, you're not looking hard enough. The point isn't to eliminate problems, but rather to create a methodical process to rapidly identify and solve them. Mature lean organizations learn how to address problems soon after they are noticed, as quickly and effectively as possible. Once the capability of daily problem solving is embedded, imagine a new environment in your company that moves from solving the crisis of the moment to solving tomorrow's problems before they occur.[15]

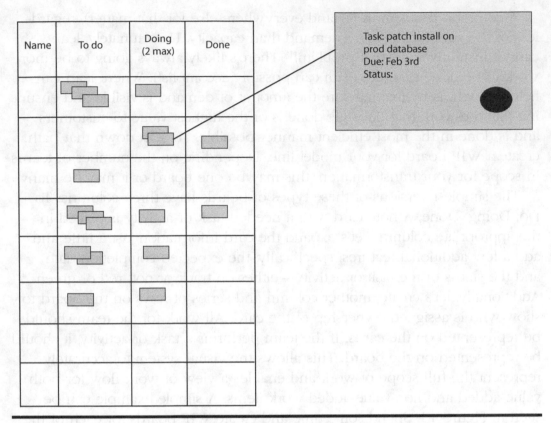

Figure 4.1 A simple WIP board that represents the total work, the prioritization and assignment of the work, and where bottlenecks are occurring.

To do this, you must create an environment where it is safe to talk about and escalate problems. We're describing a culture that rewards people for talking openly about things that are not working well instead of hiding them or creating workarounds and pretending everything is OK. Every organization has problems. A true lean organization seeks them out, makes them visible, and applies PDCA thinking to resolve them as quickly as possible.

Creating a culture focused on problem solving is a tough challenge, one that will take time and ultimately a demonstrated behavior shift in management. This section of the frontline visual management system will be used to start this cultural shift. For now, the intent is to get the team comfortable with identifying problems, making them visual, and assigning owners responsible for solving the problem. Create an area on your boards that allows for the team to post note cards or post-it notes with problems they need help with. This can be related to a current assignment, a process problem, or anything that simply isn't working as well as it should be. A key practice here is to manage WIP. Don't take on more than the team can handle. Set a WIP limit: say, two or three problems that the team will commit to actively working. Place other ideas in a holding area until an item has completed the necessary PDCA cycles and been resolved. It is much better for the team to see a few problems addressed than to see many problems in process but progress rarely achieved.

Standup Meetings

Once you have a visual representation of the work that each of the teams does, it's time to implement standup meetings. Unlike for the management team, these should occur daily and focus on tactical topics related to the work on the WIP board. The meetings should be held at the visual boards and follow a pattern used often in agile development teams. This includes ensuring equal participation by everyone on the team, quick updates lasting no longer than a total of 15 minutes for the whole team, and a focus on discussing topics important to group collaboration. Specifically, implement the standups with the following guidelines:

1. Standups occur at the visual management system for the team
2. Each member should provide a quick status of the tasks he or she is assigned and whether there are any roadblocks to the work (30–45 seconds each)
3. Each member may raise an issue or problem that he or she is struggling with or needs to escalate (just describe the *what* in 15–30 seconds)
4. Table any long discussions or problem solving until after the standup

Emphasize updates that focus on things that impact others on the team; care should be given to avoid long-winded updates best handled outside the standup meeting. The direct manager and team lead should be present at the standup meetings and encourage everyone to participate. Additionally, the manager should take any escalated problems for placement and ownership assignment on the new management boards. Only problems that the team is unable to solve should be escalated to the management board. Problems should be solved at the lowest possible level in the group whenever possible. Take care to ensure that the manager does not dominate the standup. These meetings are about team collaboration and problem identification (not solving); management has a *supporting* role in this, but associates have the *lead* role.

Standup meetings paired with visual management are an excellent place to start lean transformations for frontline associates. First, they create a higher level of accountability through the public posting of commitments as well as verbal affirmations of work status. Just as in agile teams, it's much harder to hide as a poor performer in this type of an environment. We've found that people who want to just coast and provide minimum work effort end up self-selecting out of lean teams. Second, standups allow management to gain a better understanding of the value-adding work of the front line through hearing daily the work progress and problems the staff are experiencing.

An important purpose of the lean management system is to create a direct connection between management and value-added work, and this is one of the best ways to make it happen. We'll layer in a coaching system later that will make these tools even more impactful.

Building a Purpose-Driven System

In this chapter, we have described the key components to put in place as you kick off your model line:

- ■ Basic education
- ■ Communication and collaboration
- ■ Visual management system
- ■ Standup meeting process
- ■ Transparency and connection

Using organizational purpose as a guide, all the components of this lean system are oriented toward that common theme. The impact of this method is hard to overstate! Your people will see the pieces of the puzzle (the various tools, concepts, and practices) come together as an integrated *system* where all the parts contribute to a common purpose.

To avoid confusion, let's be clear about what we mean when we use the word *system*. A system is a collection of tools, policies, practices, and procedures combined to achieve a specific goal or outcome. The components of a system are point solutions—for example, an A3 form, a standup meeting agenda, or gemba walk guidelines. Systems create the collective effect of a selected group of tools, policies, and procedures, ultimately changing the daily behavior of people.

So what behaviors do we want to drive from our lean system? Respect, engagement, enablement, enthusiasm, teamwork, openness, trust, and ownership are some of the central behaviors that are often identified. But these words mean different things to different people. What does *ideal* behavior look like? When we add a clearly articulated purpose (a True North) to the conversation, describing and modeling the specific behaviors we hope to influence through our lean system, new ways of acting and thinking become much more attainable.

An example may help here. Let's assume you are preparing for Day Zero but you have not given much thought to your True North homework from the previous chapter. Standup meetings are a key element of your model line and you are hoping to instigate some great discussions among your team members. You have a standard agenda, a visual board with measures, WIP, problems/issues, and a manager and team ready and willing to give it a try. It's like you are at the edge of the woods with a troop of people and basic hiking equipment, but without a map! If we let people just figure out the best route, we could engage in endless debate and still not necessarily select the appropriate direction to take.

So how do you know if your standup meeting discussion is focused on the right topics? How do you know if the actions and behaviors of the team are aligned with the ultimate goals of the company? There are many things they *could* focus on, but what issues *should* they focus on? Without a solid understanding and acceptance of a True North, it is a matter of opinion. Often the manager's opinion trumps the opinions of the other team members (just what we don't need—more command and control!), which has the effect of shutting people down.

Now let's take the same scenario and add a clear purpose statement: *Dedication to every client's success*. Fortified with this aim, the team could easily monitor, assess, reflect, and adjust its standup meeting by asking the simple question, "Was our focus during today's standup on the client's success?" Common agreement of purpose (our intent) acts like a set of guardrails to keep us all on track and focused on the things that matter most.

Day Zero Wrap-Up

Starting a lean journey is no easy decision. Getting started is often the most difficult step. As we progress through this field guide, we'll revisit the concepts briefly discussed here as we build a comprehensive lean system.

Implementing simple visual management and standups will create a solid foundation on which we can build and improve.

Notes

1. Gemba is defined as *the real place where work is done.*
2. The model line concept has been applied in industries as diverse as manufacturing and medicine. The magic of the concept is creating a learning lab of sorts where staff and management can see and experience lean in action. This place is also referred to as a *Dojo*—a training place (as in the martial arts).
3. A single disparaging remark from leaders and managers can do irreparable damage to the change process. It is very common that some members of leadership will be skeptical and even actively hostile toward the lean transformation. Therefore, it is important to establish clear ground rules here: All negative comments and concerns about the transformation will be kept private within the leadership team and not be shared publicly with anyone else.
4. Often the CEO and CIO are not the champions of lean IT and do not understand the critical need or potential impact it can have. It is better to work with a sponsor who understands and appreciates the core challenges and benefits of lean, so if the CIO is not onboard, go with someone who is.
5. John Shook, "How to Change a Culture: Lessons from NUMMI," *MIT Sloan Management Review*, 51(2) 64–66, 2010. See this article for an excellent read on how culture change happens and sustains in organizations.
6. Certifications can even erode credibility in the organization when the certified practitioners are unable to apply the learning in the workplace.
7. There is a tendency to shortcut this step when your management team says they can only give you 4 hours for lean orientation training. Don't make this critical error! The more comfortable the management team are with the central concepts of lean, the more they will be an enabler of the transformation.
8. We've heard many variations of the 5 feet, 3 seconds rule, but it's a powerful guideline.
9. The Shingo Prize is an award given to companies that have achieved a world-class level of Enterprise Excellence. See http://www.shingoprize.org/.
10. An A3 is a one-page report that tells a story of learning during a problem-solving cycle. See Chapter 6.
11. A common misstep we see is companies that provide massive amounts of lean training to their associates with no plan in place to apply the learning. This is a waste of time and resources and will inevitably frustrate your people and kill their enthusiasm.

12. A common complaint we hear often from those undergoing transformation is that the *facilities* group is tough to work with and won't support the changes needed. We've found it best to include the facilities group directly in discussions about the transformation. Give them a seat at the table and you'll be surprised how helpful they can be!

13. Over time, lean practices will free up work capacity by reducing wasteful activities (non-value-added work such as excessive rework).

14. We recommend that you avoid using yellow, a color reserved for *monitor*. Either we are on track or not! Red means "this needs some form of attention NOW!"

15. Credit for the concept of creating a culture that *solves tomorrow's problems* and its introduction to Tom and Nationwide is due to R. Gary Butler, Executive-in-Residence, Fisher College of Business, The Ohio State University.

Chapter 5

The Paradox of Process

An organization's ability to learn, and translate that learning into action rapidly, is the ultimate competitive advantage.

Jack Welch

Introduction

Let's be honest: You probably are not looking forward to a chapter on process. The work of IT is complicated and messy, requires judgment, and cannot simply be put into a strict process flow that dictates how we do our jobs. We've all experienced the *process police* who try to impose bureaucratic procedures that not only don't help but actually make things worse. No one wants to follow process for the purpose of process, with no real explanation of the value or because *that's just the way it is done around here*. We couldn't agree more. Unfortunately, this is the typical experience of many IT practitioners (and those that interact with and rely on IT processes). But—and this is a big but—we'd like you to keep reading and go on faith that lean process is anything but typical. Lean process enables creativity, respects people, and drives continuous improvement.

How can this be? Process is used to create a common (standard) way of doing things—how does that enable continuous improvement? It's a bit of a paradox and requires some explanation. On the one hand, lean is about experimentation and learning; on the other, we are talking about process and standardization. The question really, then, is why does one need the other? The answer is the paradox: Continuous improvement cannot exist in your organization without standardized processes. Without an accepted known starting point, an improvement is just adding to the variation and chaos of the organization. There may be a short-term improvement in performance, but without a mechanism to harvest that improvement and make it stick as a part of the ongoing processes of the organization, the real value for the company is lost. We must create a culture that views standards and processes as a way to challenge ourselves to find ways to improve the established routine and share that learning with others.

This is why lean systems care more about how you get results than the results themselves. We want results that are repeatable, not one-time heroic efforts that only apply in the moment. Not everything can be predicted in IT, but just as importantly, not everything should be random and emergent. We can use processes and systems to create predictable and stable environments from which creativity and problem solving can flourish.

People and Process

Many of you are likely familiar with the common agile mantra of *people over process*.[1] It has been used time and again to demonstrate that innovation and value come from people, not process. We do not disagree with the sentiment but think it needs further clarification; too often the statement has been used as a weapon to argue for no process. In fact, the best agile implementations are incredibly process oriented, creating predictable routines that allow teams to think creatively and solve problems.[2]

It is the combination of valuing engaged people and using process correctly that creates a high-performing system. People are at the heart of everything we do in our organizations; process enables them to have a stable environment to continually experiment with ways to deliver more value and have a more fulfilling work life. This is at the foundation of our transformation model house, represented as *Respect People*, creating an environment that allows everyone to reach his or her full potential. That has to include creating a system that wipes out chaos, fear, and ambiguity in favor of one that allows learning and growth.

How do you make this real in your transformation? Let's think about how most companies implement process. A group of *experts*, typically management, process engineers, consultants, or other staff roles that do not actually perform the work, determine an optimal (in their view) way of completing a task. The procedure is written down and stored and reviewed with staff, and the expectation is set to follow it. Then the process police audit for compliance to the standard—and look out if you're found to not be following the new standard! You'll probably be given training or advice on doing it the right way—the standard way. This all but kills process improvement because people are trained to understand deviation from the standard as a bad thing. Performance suffers as mediocrity or worse is the norm. Frontline associates grudgingly follow the process, but know there's a better way. This is not Respect for People.

On the opposite end of the spectrum, there are companies where everything appears to function extremely well. Value flows through the organization seemingly without delays or rework. Roles and responsibilities are clear and everyone pitches in toward a common goal. There is no police state enforcing process adherence, but there is a common way people do things. And when continuous improvement happens, the learning is quickly spread through the organization and the process standard is revised to reflect the new, better way.

It's the second organization that is practicing Respect for People. Lean process is not an overbearing exercise in getting people to submit. But it also is not chaos where everyone gets to do whatever he or she wants. Lean process is a baseline for continuous improvement—an acknowledgment that the current process is the best way we know how to do something right now, but that a better way can and will be found in the future. It is a statement by management that the role of everyone in the company is not to just do your job, but to find better ways of doing your job every day. Without standard process this is not possible. Paraphrasing a quote attributed to Taiichi Ohno, "Without a standard, there can be no kaizen." Indeed, without process, without what we'll call *standard work*, we cannot continuously improve.

Standard Work

Standard work is a powerful tool that you'll use to foster a culture of continuous improvement throughout your organization. Everyone in your lean IT organization will have standard work, from the CIO to the developers and every other role in between. In standard work we'll represent the critical activities and behaviors that are necessary to create value for our customers. We'll use it to drive out waste, develop people, and hold each other accountable to commitments and ongoing improvement efforts. Think of standard work not as a *common* way we do things now and forevermore, but rather as *adaptive standardization* focused on continuously improving the current standard—*standard* because everyone is expected to know and follow the process, *adaptive* because standards will change as better ways are discovered.

Both management and associates have standard work. This is not something that management inflicts on associates; it is a journey everyone will walk together. We'll refer to standard work for managers and executives as *leader standard work*. It is extremely important for you to bring the management team along with you on this journey. It's not enough for management to change the way they view the work; they must also change the way they do the work of management.

Standard Work for Associates

So what is standard work exactly? And how does it drive continuous improvement? Sometimes it's easiest to start with what something is not. Standard work is not a prescriptive set of tasks that govern the daily work of your associates from start to finish (often referred to as Standard Operating Procedures or SOPs). It is not a list of meetings to attend or a document created and owned by the management team. Standard work is the set of activities and associated behaviors that associates do to create value for customers. And standard work is what the management team will use to determine if they have created an engaging, challenging, and creative work environment or one that is onerous, bureaucratic, and stifling. The managers in your company likely don't create value directly for customers—the associates do. Standard work becomes a way to ensure that the value creators focus on value creation and managers focus on supporting them to achieve that goal.

Standard work will *not* be used as a set of instructions, referred to daily to determine what to work on. Rather, it will serve primarily as a tool for associates to strive to improve their work. It is owned by the associates and teams responsible for the work—not an external support organization or project management office (PMO). The associates' standard work isn't just for them; it is also for their managers to use for better understanding the work the associates do and to help in coaching.

The format of standard work is straightforward and can take many forms. We recommend you follow some simple rules in creating a template for use in your organization:

1. No single process can be more than one page and, preferably, will be visual using pictures, diagrams, tables, and charts.
2. Clearly show the purpose, inputs, transformation, and outputs (we like to say *outcomes*).
3. List in sequence when each process should be performed.
4. List what role should typically perform the process.

Let's take a look at each of these:

No process should be more than one page. The famous quote from Shakespeare's *Hamlet, brevity is the soul of wit,* could certainly apply to many IT process documents.[3] How many times have you been looking for information on a process only to find a virtual novel of 20 pages or more? Considering the length, you may scan it or just forget it altogether. The only people that read 20-page process documents are the people that write 20-page process documents—and they might not even read them! The greatest process in the world is of no value if it is not understood and followed. Prior to Nationwide's movement to lean software development, the development staff would joke that the cure to cancer might be buried in someone's process documents, but the world would never know because no one has time to read them![4] Don't use standard work as a weapon or a chance to show how elaborately you can document processes. In some cases there is a need for extremely detailed process flow: how to shut down a nuclear reactor, what to do if landing gear won't deploy on an airplane—but not in most cases. Even when detail is needed, use creativity to make it accessible to the staff that will use it. Only use enough words to convey key points. If you can say it with a picture or diagram, by all means do so and keep text to a minimum. Process documentation is worthless if no one pays attention to it.

Show the purpose, inputs, transformation, and outputs. For anyone that has not traveled and driven a car in the state of Oregon, in addition to the beautiful scenery, a law exists that has just about all the people who visit scratching their heads: You can't pump your own gasoline! At every gas station in the state, you pull up and are met with a sign indicating it is illegal for you to pump your own gas. Instead, you must wait for the attendant to arrive and fill up your tank. It bewilders out-of-town guests without fail (certainly it did when Tom was visiting Mike). There very well could be a good reason to deny citizens of the Beaver State the freedom to pump their own gas like the residents of every other state (except New Jersey) in the union are able to do, but no such explanation is readily available to drivers. In Tom's case, he simply ignored the rule and pumped his own gas rather than waiting on the attendant. Purpose for process is important—it's difficult to get anyone to follow a process (in the absence of threat or reward) without providing the purposeful reason for doing so. Make sure the purpose for your processes is clear and understood. If you cannot figure out what the purpose of a particular process is, ask yourself if it is really necessary.

Every process needs a purpose, and nearly every process has inputs and outputs. The work that is done by the process transforms the inputs to create the outputs. This is the most challenging part of creating effective standard work. You must answer the question, "What are the core activities that create value and what do we need to agree on concerning them?"

A weak process definition focuses only on the effort of the discrete process, without describing what the process needs to receive and the expected outcomes. Being clear on what the process needs to receive provides transparent requirements to upstream processes providing inputs. Publishing clear information on the outputs describes what downstream processes should expect to receive. Defining inputs and outputs within standard work recognizes that processes are not isolated; they are part of an interconnected system that needs all processes working together to deliver value.

Understanding inputs and outputs of the process also helps ensure quality. A tenet of lean manufacturing, known as Quality at the Source, is to not accept defects into your process or pass defects to the next process; this is similar to the familiar IT mantra of *garbage in, garbage out*. Lean IT takes the concept a step further, building quality into every step of the process.[5] Instead of testing to ensure quality, let's make the commitment to build it in right from the start through a focus on inputs, transformation, and outputs.

List when each process should be performed. Standard work should help drive the pulse of an organization. Think about the standard processes of a typical agile team. The standard work happens on a set cadence. Standups occur daily and retrospectives every 2 weeks; estimation is done at the start of each iteration, and so on. This creates a rhythm for the organization and creates a degree of predictability. Build processes that are clear and concise about when activities and tasks should occur.

List what role typically performs the process. As you build your lean organization, cross training and equipping staff to perform more than one role will be key. That's why we say to list which role *typically* performs the process. You will create collaborative teams focused on delivering value. Sometimes that requires roles to blend and the team to come together to creatively solve problems. But it is also important to understand who should be doing the process in most cases. Not having clear responsibilities or vague role definitions leads to problems and blocks understanding of the sources of waste in the value stream. Perhaps an easier way to say this is to *define the role, not the person.*

Follow these four rules when creating standard work for your associates to create processes that find the right balance of standardization, practicality, and usefulness.

Collaboratively Create Standard Work

As you craft standard work it is critically important to remember that the people who do the work, best know how to do the work. This obvious fact is often lost in translation! Standard work should not be created in isolation by external *experts*; it must be done with your associates. It's fine to bring together a small group of people from the model line to create the first iteration of your standard processes, but after the first draft, you need to solicit input from a significant portion of the organization undergoing the transformation. Use team meetings or other types of gatherings to review standard work and gather feedback. In order to demonstrate your commitment to continuous improvement and the opinions of associates, make some changes to standard work in real time in these sessions. Model the behavior of a true lean leader—don't just give continuous improvement lip service; live it.

You may not agree with all of the suggestions from your associates and some of them may not be viable, but that's OK. You are demonstrating respect to associates and showing that they now have a say in process definition and a role in shaping how the organization works. It is amazing how much engagement and buy-in is gained by simply involving the people impacted by the change. The processes will not and should not be perfect. Standard work represents an agreement between everybody that this is the way we will get the work done—until a better way is found! The magic in standard work is not that everyone is doing work the same way; rather, it's that everyone is trying to figure out a way to make the way we work better.

Let's wrap up with an example of standard work. In Chapter 4, you implemented standup meetings as an accountability practice. Let's put that practice into standard work.

Polaris Bank IT	Daily Stand Up Meeting	Version: 1.0 Effective Date: 2/3/2015

Daily Standup Standard Work

Purpose: A simple mechanism to ensure that every day starts with a daily commitment to what work will be done, a focus on any problems that exist, alignment between members of the team, and collaboration.

Figure 5.1   Start with the purpose of the standard.

Start with the purpose—What is the purpose of a standup meeting? Communication, alignment, collaboration, awareness, and commitment, all leading to increased accountability, are common themes of these types of meetings. Let's add this line of thinking to our standard work document, shown in Figure 5.1.

How about inputs—What are the inputs to a standup meeting? Standup meetings are held at the visual board, so let's call the visuals an input. And we can't hold a standup without people, so let's also add associates, team leads, and observers to the input list. What about outputs? What do we hope to get out of a standup meeting? Assignment of work items, escalated problems, ideas for improvement, and a current view of work in progress are all examples of standard outputs. The additions are shown in Figure 5.2.

Let's add in the transformational (activity) elements: timing, participants, agenda, and general work flow. See the final product in Figure 5.3.

Polaris Bank IT	Daily Stand Up Meeting	Version: 1.0 Effective Date: 2/3/2015

Daily Standup Standard Work

Purpose: A simple mechanism to ensure that every day starts with a daily commitment to what work will be done, a focus on any problems that exist, alignment between members of the team, and collaboration.

Inputs

Visual boards
Associates, team leads, observers

Outputs

Work commitments
Escalated problems
Improvement ideas
Updated visual board

Figure 5.2   Inputs and outputs.

Polaris Bank IT	Daily Stand Up Meeting	Version: 1.0 Effective Date: 2/3/2015

Daily Standup Standard Work

Purpose: A simple mechanism to ensure that every day starts with a daily commitment to what work will be done, a focus on any problems that exist, alignment between members of the team, and collaboration.

Inputs

- Visual boards
- Associates, team leads, observers

Outputs

- Work commitments
- Escalated problems
- Improvement ideas
- Updated visual board

Cadence: The daily stand up occurs daily before 10 AM and lasts no more than 15 minutes. Each team may choose a standard time when their stand up begins.

Participants: The full team. Observers are allowed but should not disrupt the flow. The team may invite other participants as they see fit.

Agenda: Each member of the team will briefly discuss work progress, problems, and daily commitment (what they will do during the rest of the day). Everyone on the team gets a turn. Team members are allowed to *pass* if they have no updates.

General Workflow: Members of the team will take turns providing updates. Only one person should speak at a time and others should listen. The team lead is responsible for noting any problems and items needing further discussion. The stand up occurs regardless of who is absent. It is a team meeting, not a status report nor a problem solving session.

Figure 5.3   A completed example of standard work for standup meetings.

As you can see, the standard work described is simple to understand and easy to create. If the team found that they were not consistently discussing and then capturing improvement ideas on their visual board, they might add a call out in the standard work highlighting the need to perform this process step daily. Creating process in this way sets expectations for associates and, at the same time, gives them the freedom to innovate and improve. The process of developing standard work also builds the foundation of a culture of transparency. For your staff, this can be both empowering and frightening at the same time. Take the time throughout your transformation to address these fears and position standard work as a tool to drive improvement instead of as a weapon to enforce adherence. In Chapter 6, you will spend some time on this and create a system to enable associates to rapidly and perpetually improve standard work.

Standard Work for Leaders

When we refer to *Lead with Respect*, we're talking about demonstrating through action your belief that everyone has a contribution to make and a right to work in an environment where he or she can be successful based on the level of engagement and teamwork. The ultimate role of leadership is to create a workspace where people are able to grow to new levels of performance. This is accomplished by embracing a new understanding of respect. Respect in this sense is about seeing the best in people and the constrained and dormant talent that needs to be freed. A key role of a leader is to develop people to unleash that potential!

With this in mind, how does standard work apply to leaders? There is a difference in the purpose of standard work and leader standard work. In standard work for associates, the focus is directly placed on value-added activities—enabling them to be more focused and effective. Leader standard work also focuses on the value-added work, but through the execution of management activities centered on actively supporting the frontline associates and sustaining the momentum of the lean system.

Think of it this way: The teams and associates are the people driving the car (creating value) while the managers and leaders are the pit crew whose job it is to support their drivers to successfully navigate the track. Neither can be successful without the support of the other and both must be successful in their roles for the other to have success!

Many lean deployments focus only on the front line. Zeroing in on the activities that directly interface with customers can quickly create greater value. Unfortunately, without a corresponding management system that reinforces frontline systems, improvements won't stick and the transformation is doomed. Your associates will take the lead from their managers (and your managers will take their cues from their bosses); if lean is important to the management team, it will be important to them. If it's not, then lean will be viewed as just the next flavor of the month improvement program that will eventually die out. Leader standard work creates the cadence of activities and behaviors needed for sustainability.

We prefer the term *leader* standard work instead of *manager* standard work because the focus is on actions of a lean leader, not the administrative tasks of a manager that, while sometimes necessary, do not serve to sustain lean improvements. Both management and leadership are necessary competencies of a successful management team. But being a manager does not automatically make you a leader. Regrettably, many companies equate the two. We've experienced many managers that are wonderful leaders, as well as managers unable to demonstrate true leadership. Leaders create an environment that allows associates to grow and contribute to the success of the company. Leadership does not mean telling people what to do; it's about engaging and inspiring people to do the right thing without having to tell them what to do!

While the standard work you created for associates was very tactical and focused on how work gets done, leader standard work takes on different form and function. For leaders you'll create a simplified document that outlines the cadence of activities and behaviors they will be held accountable for performing. There will be common elements among leaders in the organization, but each leader will have his or her own standard work, a personal version reviewed regularly with the boss.

A few simple guidelines to help you create the documents include the following:

1. Focus on activities and behaviors that demonstrate leading with respect.
2. Make associate development and coaching a central theme.
3. The higher the level of the manager, the more strategic the focus will be.

Let's examine each of these:

■ *Focus on activities and behaviors.* For your leaders, less emphasis is placed on process definition than for the associates. Don't worry too much about inputs and outputs, but do focus deeply on purpose. The *intent* (the *why*) of management and leadership actions is incredibly important. What are the activities that will sustain the lean system? What activities will drive better performance at the front line? How does a leader model the behaviors expected of the staff? These should be guiding questions in defining the activities and behaviors we wish to see. A simple example of this type of leader standard work is attendance at the management team standup meetings. If you believe that the management standups drive accountability and problem solving, set the expectation with the model line management team of attendance (activity) and participation (behavior) of everyone on the management team.

■ *Associate development and coaching.* Above all else, the job of a lean leader is to develop people. The true value of a company is not created in the executive suite; it's created day in and day out by the people in the trenches creating value for customers—the frontline staff. It's amazing how many managers don't get this fact and spend little to no time actively coaching and developing the very people that will ultimately determine the success of their organization. In fairness, most managers already put coaching at the top of their priority list. But rarely does that translate into action. Ask some of the staff at your company whether or not they have meaningful coaching relationships with their manager, and most will reference a quarterly or annual review process. Lean coaching occurs daily, on the spur of the moment, and focuses on teaching associates how to problem solve autonomously. A lean leader's job is not to solve problems; rather, it's to teach others how to solve problems, unleashing their creativity and passion. That doesn't happen looking at a spreadsheet or attending meetings; it happens at the gemba in daily interaction with staff.

One of the best ways to ensure that this kind of coaching happens regularly is the addition of a simple entry in every manager's standard work: a weekly review with each of his subordinates discussing their standard work. This creates a simple *check* of standard work within the PDCA cycle. It ensures that each manager (1) understands and follows standard work, (2) is focusing on continuous improvement and coaching, and (3) has a regular venue to talk about any problems related to the current processes. Standard work requires more care and feeding than traditional process management, but with this simple check, it is much more powerful.

A deviation from this standard work review pattern is necessary for frontline managers and their teams. Managers should also have regular discussions with associates, but it should be done at the gemba in the form of daily spontaneous coaching opportunities rather than direct standard work reviews. As much as possible, make coaching for performance and development of the frontline staff an activity that occurs at the gemba. This practice has the added benefit of reinforcing the practice of getting managers out from behind their desks and to the place where the work is done.

■ *The higher the level of the manager, the more strategic the standard work*. The views of the organization by the front line and by the executive are different. All managers, regardless of level, need to have a connection to the value-adding processes of the front line. Executive managers need to possess a broader view and have the perspective and vision to articulate where the company needs to be heading. Frontline associates have the know-how to create value and solve daily problems. In many companies, executives micromanage the *how*, hoping to engage people. But command-and-control tactics only make matters worse and result in poor communication and associates who don't trust management. Leader standard work addresses these issues head-on by emphasizing a daily connection with the people doing the work. The daily intensity and commitment to the process of that connection is what differs based on the level of the manager.

Frontline managers' standard work should be more tactically focused: going to the gemba daily to coach for development, reviewing visuals, and so on. A direct, daily connection with their teams and the work being done by them is essential. The managers' standard work ensures a focus on this connection and helps counterbalance against the constant interruptions and distractions that happen throughout the day. Without a tool such as standard work, the important work of getting to gemba and coaching is often supplanted by the perceived urgency of e-mail, reports, and fire-fighting drills.

For more senior-level managers, the level of daily interaction diminishes by design. The connection to the *real work* of the front line is vitally important to these executives. Strategic decisions can't effectively be made without this connection; however, there are other important tasks as well, such as strategy reviews and long-term planning. It's important to not allow strategic activities to prevent senior leadership from visiting the gemba and understanding the tactical work the associates perform. Build gemba walks and visits to team-level standups,[6] and associate interactions into the standard work of executives to ensure that it remains a focus.

Leader Standard Work in Practice

The lean journey for your managers is more personal than for the associates. While there are many common elements across management—such as visual management and standups—there are also elements that are unique to each manager. For example, there might be a specific callout in standard work for the VP of development to frequently attend show-and-tells[7] of agile teams, whereas the VP of infrastructure might need to attend less frequently. The focus is customized to each executive.

Leader standard work takes a different format from what you created for your associates. Figure 5.4 shows a sample document for an IT Director. Notice a focus on activities and behaviors, along with how frequently they should be performed. There is less emphasis on traditional process flow, and more emphasis on the expectations and *intent* of leadership.

Get started with your own leader standard work for the model line. What behaviors are important for your management team to model? What expectations should be set for lean leaders in your organization?

Polaris Bank
Application Development Director
Version 1.0: 12/30/2013

Daily	Intent
1. Attend daily Tier II standup	Escalations, Improvements, Commitments
2. Address any escalated issues – directly or escalate	Ensure high productivity and engagement
3. Gemba Walk to each team space	Understand the work, coach, connect, demonstrate commitment to the lean system
4. Identify one coaching opportunity	Learn and teach

Weekly	Intent
1. Project meetings	Strategic and tactical input; Risk and issue management
2. 1:1 Coaching (directs, project team members)	Ensure high productivity and engagement; Review standard work
3. A3 Reviews – owned and sponsored	Keep commitments; Coach
4. Social media	Connect with associates the way they want

Monthly	Intent
1. Development planning	Engagement (Career development of associates)
2. Succession planning (meet with potential candidates)	Career development
3. Tools & technology research	Tool & technology continuous improvement
4. Update app dev roadmap	Practice strategic planning

Figure 5.4   Notice the difference in focus of leader standard work.

People-Centric Process

We began this chapter talking about process as a paradox. There is an indispensible tension that exists between stability and change, and information technology has forgotten the link between the two. Process has become a dirty word to some. Our business partners think our processes are heavy handed and prevent rapid adaptation to a changing business climate. Frontline staff think processes are created as a measuring stick and prevent innovation. And managers are tired of being the *process police*. Use lean process to change the rules of the game.

Standard work focuses processes on what they were meant to be: a baseline of practice and a way to continuously innovate, develop and grow our staff, and create competitive advantage for our companies. Take the time to begin creating standard work for your associates and managers in the model line transformation.

Notes

1. The actual wording, *individuals and interactions over processes and tools*, can be found at http://www.agilemanifesto.org/.
2. The difference in agile processes is they are geared toward empowerment rather than control.
3. An irony often lost in the use of this quote is that it was uttered by Lord Polonius, perhaps the least witty and longest-winded of all the characters in the play. It's illustrative even to this day: The creators of these paper processes often are stating things they cannot back up. If your processes are created in isolation of the people that have to use them, something is wrong.
4. Nationwide moved from a process that would routinely create 20+ page requirements documents to a process that encouraged the creation of high-level requirements followed by visual management of requirements through the use of a common agile tool, story cards. The long documents became a rallying cry for the staff of a new centralized IT organization called the Application Development Center to demonstrate the waste inherent in the current process.
5. Lean Manufacturing has also embraced building quality in at the start, but the IT community has taken the practice even further with integrated testing and continuous deployment practices.
6. There is no easier way to reinforce the importance of the lean system to your associates than to have your executive team demonstrate visible and active support for lean practices such as standups, visual management, reflections, and gemba walks.
7. A show-and-tell is a fairly standard agile practice where teams demo the working software they created during the prior development cycle, typically a 2- to 4-week interval.

Chapter 6

Problem-Solving Scientists

> If I had an hour to solve a problem I'd spend 55 minutes thinking
> about the problem and 5 minutes thinking about solutions.
>
> **Albert Einstein**

Introduction

For the purposes of this chapter, please assume you know nothing about
problem solving and read on as if it were all sparkling new information for
you to process! This may seem like a strange request, but here's why:

Anyone who has read about lean and process improvement has almost
certainly come across lofty aspirations such as "Creating a Culture of
Continuous Improvement and Problem Solving!" and "We're a Learning
Organization." That's all well and good, but rarely do we find anything close
to this when visiting companies. As an assessor for the Shingo Institute,[1]
Mike has had the opportunity to visit many organizations that are motivated
to transform their culture to achieve Enterprise Excellence. Some of these
organizations are quite impressive and have made great strides. That said,
the area that often lags in terms of progress is the widespread adoption of
problem-solving *behaviors* by people at all levels of the organization. We
find this surprising since problem solving is such a central theme in lean,
Six Sigma, and other process improvement practices. What's more, problem
solving has been the main focus of improvement initiatives for the past three
decades, yet we really aren't that good at it!

Why is this the case? Here's our take: Most people see themselves as natural problem solvers. They have spent their lives solving problems: at school, at home, at work; "All I do is solve problems!" is a common retort. People see themselves as capable problem solvers already understanding and possessing problem-solving skills and thus assume, "I know this stuff." But are we really *effective* problem solvers? Or are we jumping to solutions based on our biases and presumptions about what we think we know? Problem solving is not about starting with a solution and then creating a justification; rather, it is the application of a methodical progression to deeply understand current state and root cause, test potential countermeasures, and adapt based on the results.

Brian Hinken describes this well as being a *learner* and not a *knower*.[2] Only when we allow ourselves to acknowledge that we don't know the answer, that we all have more to learn, do we begin to embrace a problem-solving mindset. This is much more difficult to do than it sounds. We have been conditioned as humans to recognize and reward—even envy and idolize—those who have the answers, the crazy geniuses and other naturally *smart* people. It takes time and courage to create a culture that rewards the opposite: knowing we don't understand deeply enough to have the answer but being willing to struggle, learn, and discover it.[3]

Think back to grade school: The teacher asks students to raise their hands if they *know* the answer—not if they are *unsure* of the answer. Most people want to raise their hands and may think they know the answer, but we're missing an important point. Learning is much less about having a specific answer and more about the process of expanding our understanding to move to a deeper awareness of the situation we are trying to change. This significantly impacts how we should be teaching, coaching, and working with our co-workers. If you respect your people and want to build a culture of continuous improvement, move away from asking people for *solutions* and begin to ask open-ended questions that develop their problem-solving skills.

When you're in a *solutions* frame of mind, you don't give the topic the attention necessary to deeply understand, let alone master, the mindset and skill set needed to be a really good problem solver. But when you are in a discovery frame of mind, the role of a manager becomes that of a coach who uses questions to position the learner to expand their understanding of a condition to better understand cause and effect.

The kind of problem solving we explore in this chapter is very different from what most people think of as everyday problem solving—it's a structured and standardized approach to the way we think about obstacles and strive to understand cause and effect. In our opinion, it is the *simplicity* of the lean problem-solving model that actually hinders our ability to use it to solve problems! The outward uncomplicatedness of the lean problem-solving model reinforces people's perception that they already understand everything they need to know about it. Just because something is simple to describe does not mean that it is easy to do!

What Is a Problem?

This may seem like an obvious question and hardly worthy of discussion, but we find that most people have not really given this topic much thought and that clarity around what a problem is (and isn't) is very useful when attempting to solve one! A problem is a situation where (a) there is dissatisfaction by customers, employees, and/or suppliers in the way things work today; or (b) a current process contains waste (non-value-added[4] steps), an unacceptable degree of variation, or overburden; and (c) no one has a clear and complete understanding of the cause(s) of the current condition. For our purposes, for a problem to exist, we have frustration, or a wasteful process, and lack a clear and complete understanding of the reasons why.[5] If that is the case, action needs to be taken in the form of an experiment to clarify and deepen our understanding of the problem and potential countermeasures. But let's not get ahead of ourselves.

Lean can be defined in many ways, but above all, it is a *system of learning* and a *system of respect*. The ultimate purpose of lean and continuous process improvement is to develop great learning organizations with the intention of delivering value to all stakeholders (customers, employees, shareholders, suppliers, community). Great learning organizations achieve high levels of performance and sustain it even when environments change.[6] In fact, learning capability becomes an insurmountable competitive advantage because it takes time and hard work to develop! If you have a few years head start on your competitors in learning and applying problem solving and you make it part of your daily work, it is very difficult if not impossible for competitors to catch up; they have to go through the same sometimes-painful trials of learning new ways of thinking and behaving. There is no shortcut to learning lean problem solving—but there is a well-worn path you can follow!

There is a classic story of Toyota Loom Works where a blueprint for an automatic loom was stolen. This was technology the company had developed after years of hard work and created a significant competitive advantage at the time. When it was discovered that the plans had been stolen, the people remained composed and realized they were already further ahead in their learning than anything the blueprint could show. The realization was that it was the learning process, not the specific knowledge, which created an advantage in the marketplace. Toyota continues to share the Toyota Production System model with the world, in part because the company realizes that no one can catch up in terms of learning!

ENDS VERSUS MEANS

You may be reading this and thinking, "How can the ultimate goal of lean (and lean IT) be learning and respect? Aren't those just a means to an end—delivering stable technology which enables my company to deliver the right products and services?" That is what we call a *two-bottles-of-wine conversation*! All too often we see companies, whose singular focus is on results, effectively ignoring the means by which results are achieved. The reason we stress learning and respect before value creation is simple: these elements must be in place before we begin to realize even the smallest of the rewards they produce.

Outcomes are important to be sure, but when we focus exclusively on them, they become increasingly elusive and difficult to achieve because we distort our focus on the primary intention. The main target is small step improvement based on experimentation; the results are a by-product. When we focus solely on the outcomes, especially in an environment that doesn't value respect for people, we often reward sociopaths who see people as a consumable to achieve their goals. We both incent and reward the wrong behavior, which is a downward spiral compounding itself.

By making the means the primary focus, results are achieved. This may seem counterintuitive, but we all become what we think about and dwell on most frequently. To generate great results, we need the right behavior—learning and respect are two key elements. When talking about lean with your team, stressing behaviors more and talking less about the outcomes will bring about the changes that need to take place. If they understand the direction (the "what"), the reason (the "why") and are empowered with the right tools and support, they won't just deliver, but will develop habits of learning and more easily adapt to change.

People Focus

To achieve great results, we need stable and capable processes, and for process stability we need engaged, enabled, and enthusiastic people. It is people and only people who run, tinker, adjust, and improve their work methods in order to deliver value to customers. If people are the drivers of process improvement, then lean is ultimately about developing people. This is worth repeating: *lean is a learning system* and we learn best and most quickly by solving problems that directly impact us. That is why this chapter is so important to you and your company!

Unfortunately, you can't really learn problem solving by reading about it. People have to practice, and the more they do, the better they get! Again, these ideas are easy to describe and deceptively difficult to actuate at both personal and organizational levels. There are numerous books on lean problem solving[7] and reading them can provide insights and understanding, but they are not an effective substitute for the constructive tension that is caused when people address real challenges where the work is done and value created, at the gemba.

To learn a new habit, Mike likes to say, "It takes 40 days to make it and another 40 days to own it."[8] So if you are serious about embedding problem solving into your organization's daily work, people need to practice every day for 3 months for it to begin to take hold. Later, we'll talk about work systems that you can leverage to reinforce daily team-based problem solving so that the practice becomes a seamless part of work (people will be learning and they may not even be aware of it!). By the way, we are talking about 80 *consecutive* days of applying lean problem solving. If you miss a day, the next day is day one and you start the 80-day count from the beginning. This simple technique encourages people to *keep up* with a daily routine until it sinks in and becomes habit.

Who Wants to Be a Scientist?

Lean problem solving is all about applying the Scientific Method[9] to address problems and opportunities in our daily work. One challenge is that most people don't like to talk about, let alone deal with, problems. Problems have a negative connotation in the workplace, so when the boss asks, "Do you have any problems?" people choose to respond, "No problems here!" There are many reasons for this: our education

(A = good; F = bad), the stigma of making a mistake, possible judgment by others for not solving problems on your own, and the meddling that comes from your boss if you admit to having a problem, just to name a few.

Imagine what your culture would be like if people came to work not only to do their work, but also to find better ways to do their work. Instead of simply being an *employee*, every staff member is a problem-solving scientist who is not afraid to make mistakes, knowing that learning from errors and surprises is the key to greater understanding.

Thomas Edison, the man often credited with inventing the electric light bulb,[10] struggled with his team of scientists to discover the filament that would successfully conduct DC current inside a light bulb. In an interview, he was asked, "Aren't you discouraged by failing so many times in your attempt to successfully invent the electric light bulb?" Edison reportedly replied, "I have not failed 10,000 times. I have successfully found 10,000 ways that will not work." We love this story because it captures the essence of scientific thinking. It is not about trial and *error*; instead it is all about trial and *discovery*. We learn from our setbacks as well as, and perhaps more than, from our successes. Learning happens through failure. It is persistence and the practice of a pattern of steps that lie at the essence of lean problem solving. Let's see what those are.

Plan–Do–Check–Adjust (PDCA)

The lean problem-solving methodology is divided into four stages: Plan, Do, Check, Adjust.[11] At each step of the process, there is an opportunity to reflect and learn using micro PDCA cycles,[12] as we shall see. Figure 6.1 shows the PDCA cycle along with a brief description of each component. Although simplistic at first encounter, this model is amazingly powerful at driving methodical learning and effective problem solving. Let's look at the main components:

Plan

The objective of this initial step is to understand and deeply perceive what is currently happening in the work process. What are the people doing? What information and material flows are taking place? What is the gap between what should be happening and what is happening? What is working and what is broken? Does the process flow smoothly? What kinds of problems are occurring and where? Where are the problems occurring and what is their nature? What else is there to know about the real story? This step is often

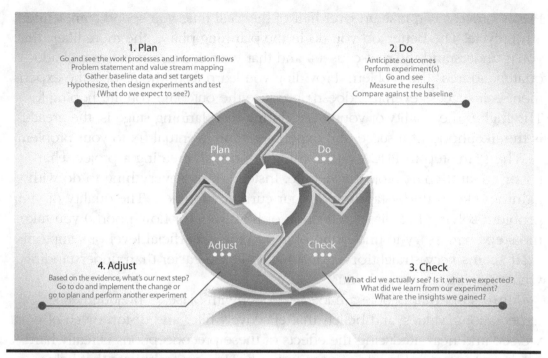

1. Plan
Go and see the work processes and information flows
Problem statement and value stream mapping
Gather baseline data and set targets
Hypothesize, then design experiments and test
(What do we expect to see?)

2. Do
Anticipate outcomes
Perform experiment(s)
Go and see
Measure the results
Compare against the baseline

Plan
•••

Do
•••

Adjust
•••

Check
•••

4. Adjust
Based on the evidence, what's our next step?
Go to do and implement the change or
go to plan and perform another experiment

3. Check
What did we actually see? Is it what we expected?
What did we learn from our experiment?
What are the insights we gained?

Figure 6.1   The PDCA model.

referred to as *grasp the situation*. The primary method you need to use here is *Go and See*, which means to go where the work is happening and where the problem is occurring to see firsthand with your own eyes what is going on.

This sounds reasonable, but most people (including the authors) have to break through the baggage of past experience and internal assumptions to (1) go and see, and then (2) *really see* what is there! Taichi Ohno, considered the father of the Toyota Production System,[13] said, "Don't look with your eyes, look with your feet. Don't think with your head, think with your hands." You have to break away from the comfort of your cube or office and get out to where the real work is happening. Even if that means logging onto a program and walking through a work process with staff members by stepping through an application, then do it; if it means getting out to the data center or visiting a development team, then do it—IT managers are not exempt from going to the gemba!

Planning includes understanding the process that you want to improve, explaining the business impact of the current state, identifying what may be causing the problem, identifying what needs to change and how we can measure it, performing deeper analysis to understand root cause, and identifying possible countermeasures and experiments we can do to better understand and validate their efficacy. When performed to the right level, this step of the

PDCA process can take up over half of the total time you spend completing a full cycle! The better job you do in the planning phase, the more likely that you'll understand the root cause(s) and that your countermeasures will adequately address the problem. Providing you learn from the results, the experiment is a success even if it doesn't produce the outcome you are hoping for. The higher the quality of your work during the planning stage is, the greater is the likelihood of a successful experiment and eventual fix to your problem.

The Plan step in PDCA has nothing to do with creating a project charter or a Gantt chart project schedule. Instead, it has everything to do with gaining a keen understanding of your current condition. The quality of your problem solving is a direct reflection of how well (or how poorly) you take the steps necessary to understand beyond the superficial level of symptoms. It all seems very straightforward: What could be easier than understanding what is going on around you?

It turns out that people are loaded down with biases,[14] prejudgments, expectations, values, and beliefs that effectively filter and distort much of what we see and hear. Reducing the effects of these preconceptions is really hard work and you need to take it very seriously. Here's a technique that helps: When you go and see, imagine you are seeing people, systems, and work processes for the first time. Adopt a beginner's frame of mind and assume you know nothing about the work process you are investigating. This will take awareness and humility on your part to do it effectively. The more you can get outside yourself, the easier it is to see what is really happening. Like everything else we are discussing, this takes practice, practice, and more practice!

Do

This stage is all about running a *single factor* experiment and comparing the results to the expectations you recorded in the Plan stage of the learning cycle. Perhaps the most common mistake we see (and made for years!) is to make multiple changes to a process at the same time. With this approach, there is no way to know which countermeasures have helped and which have hurt your improvement effort.

Before you perform your experiment, here are a few things you need to do:

■ In the Planning stage, identify and document the countermeasures the team is considering. Years ago, Mike had a coach who challenged him to identify seven countermeasures before going forward. This is tough;

most people can come up with two or three without even going to the gemba, but after that, you really need to stretch your thinking to come up with seven potential improvements you can seriously suggest!

■ An important practice here is to write things down. Don't rely on memory when doing this next step in the PDCA cycle. Someone once said, "If you only plan to see what happens, you will." You need to write out your prediction, as follows: "If we do x, we expect to get y." This deceptively powerful statement captures your prediction of what you expect to see happen and sets you up for learning regardless of the outcome of the experiment. This is the essence of the scientific method.[15]

■ A great question to ask yourself and the team is, "What is the smallest thing we could do to impact the problem?" This simple question often frees up people's minds to include seemingly insignificant changes. Lean problem solving is all about making many small-step improvements versus hitting the jackpot with a single countermeasure that is the panacea to all our problems! Teams are often paralyzed by what they perceive to be the size of the task at hand. This approach supports people breaking problems into small, actionable pieces and making real progress they can build on.

■ For each countermeasure, identify the problem, possible root cause(s), and a measurement that will be impacted, and guess how much it will move. It is important to answer the question, "How will we confirm the impact of the change we are making?" This step also stretches our thinking and learning by positioning our minds to be open to discovery, no matter the results of the experiment. It's also a good idea to ask, "What do we expect to learn as a result of this experiment?"

Check

Now it's time to begin deep learning by comparing the results of our experiment to our expectations (which we wrote down) and to see what they teach us. This step is critical to learning and it is entirely based on *confirming* our hunches and ideas. If you don't like the words *hunch*, or *guess*, or *intuition*, then use *hypothesis*. As we said earlier, this practice is the scientific method and based entirely on validated learning. One of four outcomes can occur:

1. The results match our expectations. This happens less often than we like, but when it does, it suggests we have a good understanding of

cause and effect and that our countermeasure has a positive impact on the problem we are attempting to solve.

2. The results do not match our expectations. This is often the outcome of our first few experiments as we begin to realize we really don't understand the process and problems deeply enough to make a measurable improvement. At times, there is no effect or a measurable negative impact as a result of the experiment. The needle does not move at all! This can be demoralizing to the team if we don't manage expectations, be honest and open about where we are in the learning process, and lead with respect. The important thing to do here is to ask ourselves, "Could this be the result of our not measuring the right thing or inaccurately measuring it?" "Do we understand both the root cause and the countermeasure deeply enough to make sense of the outcome we are witnessing?"

3. The results are positive, but only partially match our expectations. In other words, we have some improvement that we can confirm, but not enough. We haven't moved the dial far enough, so what's our next step?

Adjust

Our final stage of the learning cycle is to react appropriately based on the discoveries made in the previous Check step. Think evidenced-based action when performing this step. Based on the results of the experiment, your next step should be

1. If the results of the experiment match our expectations and make a positive confirmable improvement, the next step is to identify how you will mobilize and spread the change so that it becomes embedded in the standard work process. What needs to change for the countermeasure to become the shared way we do the work? Who needs to know? What needs to be different in the work environment to support the change? What new behaviors need to be established? What triggers need to be put into play to begin to make this a habit? See Chapter 5 for information on standard work.

2. If the results for your experiment do not confirm what the team expected, then ask yourself, "What are the facts telling us and what do they tell us about our level of understanding of cause and effect?" When you are at this point in the learning cycle, there is naturally some disappointment and frustration because we all tend to assume we understand what is happening and are confident that our countermeasures will work.

The next step is to take the learning from the last experiment, reflect and discuss, and then enter another cycle of PDCA with a renewed level of understanding! This takes discipline and tenacity because it is so much easier to give up and say, "It's out of our hands, way too complicated, and beyond our circle of control!" Don't cave in; this is a conscious choice you and your team need to make. In fact, it is the strength of the team that directly impacts the quality of your countermeasures because the best ideas emerge from high levels of collaboration and trust.

3. If the results are good, but not good enough, the team needs to consider whether they should go forward with the partially effective countermeasure and then proceed with another cycle of PDCA or place the working improvement aside, do another PDCA cycle, and then consider integrating the two. The decision you make should be based on the team's shared thinking. This is where a good coach can play a key role in developing the learner's judgment and critical thinking skills. The situation is also a great opportunity to build trust and respect among team members as you explore your options.

4. If the experiment has no impact or a negative influence on the problem, a new round of PDCA is clearly the next step to take. However, before you do, the team needs to ask the same questions to clearly identify the learning and discovery gained from the last trial. It is not enough to say, "Well that didn't work, so let's pick another countermeasure and try that."

As we mentioned earlier, at each step of the process there is an opportunity to reflect and learn using rapid micro PDCA cycles. Think of it this way: As you move from one stage of the learning cycle to the next, ask yourself the following questions: What did I learn and what do I know now? How do I know it? What else do I need to know? Where and with whom can I go and see to deepen my understanding? Am I prepared to go to the next step in the PDCA process?

Hopefully, you are beginning to see that lean problem solving is essentially a very effective system of learning. By honoring the PDCA process daily, the key skill we are developing in our people is the acquisition of process knowledge. We like to use the term *honor* as it implies a code of behavior and respect for people. If we honor the PDCA process, we avoid lazy thinking that comes from taking shortcuts and avoiding work we're not comfortable doing.

Your Brain on A3

Putting PDCA into action is the next step on your transformation journey. Unfortunately you cannot just flip a switch and have everyone in your company become an expert problem solver. A tool is needed to begin to build the daily behavior that makes problem solving a daily habit. The A3 is a simple-to-use method for building the problem-solving muscle of your organization. Done well, it will become the currency of continuous improvement and process changes in the organization.

The A3 Template

The A3 is a one-page form used to reinforce the PDCA thinking process. Very much like the PDCA process itself, the form is deceptively simple and belies the challenging brainwork that lies ahead for the person or teams filling it in. There are numerous A3 templates available on the web,[16] and they all do a pretty good job of compartmentalizing thinking into the PDCA elements. The term A3 simply refers to the size of the paper using a European standard, 11 inches × 17 inches. An example A3 template can be seen in Figure 6.2.

A great A3 tells a story about a problem or process change. How often have you wondered about the thinking behind why a process is the way it is? What if you had a way to look back at changes made to see why a certain approach was taken? A3s give you that ability. At their best, A3s provide a narrative of the thought processes and reasoning in problem solving and

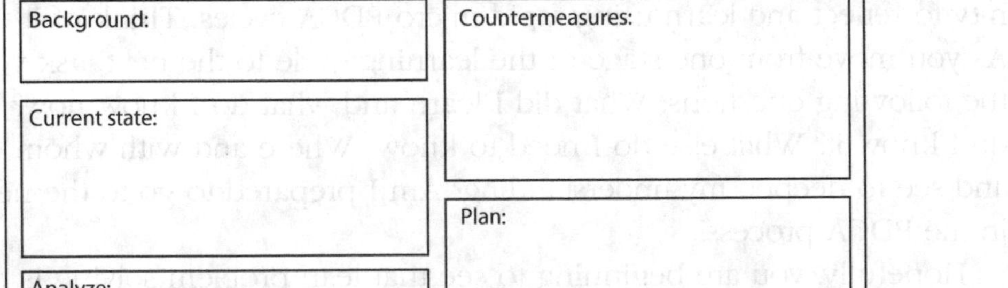

Figure 6.2   Example A3 template.

process change. In fact, you may have noticed that we've been referring to problem solutions as *countermeasures* for the simple fact that very few solutions are ever permanent.

Even more important than looking backward at process changes, the A3 is a way to affect PDCA thinking by providing an account of the progression of learning that takes place as the team follows a PDCA learning cycle. It gives you a straightforward process to affect behavioral change in your transformation. Let's take a more detailed look at the A3 and then circle back to implementation in your model line.[17]

Background/Problem Statement

Why should we care?

- What is the problem we are trying to solve?
- Why is it important?
- How was the problem discovered?

This section is your chance to grab the attention of the reader, to make him or her want to keep reading. Frame the problem such that the decision makers can understand why something needs to be done. (What is the impact to the business? How will this affect our customers?) It doesn't matter how smart you sound if your countermeasures are never implemented.

Current Condition/Current State

How is the system currently operating? What is the impact of this problem (think safety, quality, delivery time, productivity, customer satisfaction, morale, revenue, profits, reputation, etc.)?

- What are the specific symptoms and who is feeling them?
- Can we show the problem's size and behavior in terms of a measure using a trend line, pie chart, Pareto analysis,[18] or some other visual?
- Can we observe the problem with our own eyes?

Current state is just that: Describe the system or problem as it is today—not the ideal path or what the process documentation says, but rather as you observe it operating (e.g., "We observed that 20% of the jobs are being reworked for data accuracy and completeness").

Analysis and Understanding

What do we understand about the current condition?

- What *should* be happening and what *is* happening?
- What is preventing us from moving to an improved target condition?[19]
- What is our current understanding of specific cause and effect?
- Are dependencies clear and understood?
- Do all of the steps in the process add value?
- What is stopping the flow of information or material?

This section is your chance to put your detective skills to use. Appropriate tools often used in Analysis are cause maps, fishbone diagrams, Pareto charts, 5 Whys, histograms, and control charts. Incidentally, this is often the section new A3 practitioners rush through as they are confident they already know the answer.

Target/Objectives/Goals

What is the desired outcome?

- What needs to be different for things to be better, right now?
- What is a baseline measurement we can capture before we make any changes?
- How can we measure success before and after the countermeasure is taken?

Be as specific as possible with your goals. Don't just say, "Improve the performance of the database" or something similar. What specifically constitutes better performance? If the goals are too far out in the future (e.g., ideal future condition), set intermediate goals (e.g., target condition).

To avoid losing the interest of the organization, ensure that you have goals achievable within 30 to 90 days. We have found that shorter rapid cycles of learning bring about better results and higher levels of engagement. Challenge teams to perform small experiments (hours or days) versus large projects (weeks or months). The smaller the countermeasure is, the easier it is to test. The faster the experiment is to test, the quicker the learning will be.

Proposed Countermeasures

What do we want to do to make an improvement?

■ What are our proposed countermeasures? (Try to identify seven!)
■ How did we select the *one* we want to try first?
■ Have we drawn a clear connection between our suggested countermeasure and a root cause?
■ How will we know if a change is an improvement?

Selected countermeasures should be able to be traced directly to a root cause of the problem and must be able to be implemented. A countermeasure does no good if it is too difficult to execute or does not have the support of the people responsible for the process.

Implementation Plan

What is the plan?

■ What are the tasks, responsibilities, deliverables, and due dates needed to implement the countermeasure?
■ What challenges and risks do we anticipate and need to watch for?
■ Have we defined some measures of success? Are these the same measures we identified earlier (target/objectives/goals)? If not, why have they changed?

The plan is all about the *who, what,* and *when* required to implement the countermeasures. The method to manage the implementation can vary from traditional Gantt charts to story cards to milestones.

Sustaining Measures and Follow-Up

If this works, how do we sustain the gains and continue to get better?

■ When are we scheduled to perform a checkup to see if things are really better? How often will we check?
■ How will we know if the countermeasure had the impact needed?
■ How do we ensure that our learning is shared with others?
■ If the countermeasure is effective, how will we sustain it?

The follow-up section often receives short shrift, but that's a huge mistake. Don't assume everything is fine simply because you took all the right steps in defining the problem, finding root cause, and methodically implementing countermeasures. Periodically, you need to check to ensure that things are still working well, take the time to bake the process changes into standard work, and anticipate that other countermeasures will be needed in the future—because they will be!

The A3 in Action

Once you have a solid understanding of A3s, put them into action in the model line. Commit to it; A3 is the tool you will use for problem solving. It is the primary mechanism to create world-class problem solvers in your company. If you don't understand the problem's cause and effect, you need an A3. Even if you think you do understand cause and effect, the process of filling out an A3 can capture the team's reasoning as to why they took the actions they chose and be used to gain buy-in, share the learning, and document the thinking.

Use A3s with both management and associates to solve problems that are larger than *just do it* type issues. If someone wants to move the water cooler from an isolated corner of the building to where everyone is located, that probably doesn't need an A3. If your primary website cannot handle the traffic on Monday mornings despite someone working on it for 6 months, that probably (most definitely!) does need an A3. If it is unclear why managers are not going on their gemba walks, create an A3. You get the point—practice A3 *thinking* until it becomes a part of the DNA of the organization.

Some rules to keep in mind as you get started include:

1. One owner of the A3. This individual can be chosen for a variety of reasons, but one person is ultimately responsible for its creation.
2. A qualified coach and sponsor. Someone has to be able to coach those new to the A3 process—what it is, why it is used, and how. The sponsor needs to have the authority to approve selected countermeasure experimentation and implementation.
3. Go to the gemba. It may sound redundant at this point, but get out from behind your desk and get to where the real work happens. A3s

should not be created in isolation. Talk to the people involved in the process or problem—build consensus.
4. Use pencil and paper. In fairness, no one in IT ever listens to this rule. The intent is that the A3 is created and modified as you learn. We like pencil and paper, but a computer is fine as long as you realize that the A3 will change often. If you must create the A3 electronically, take a printout with you to the gemba.
5. Use pictures and drawings. Don't worry about your artistic abilities. Simple drawings and pictures convey meaning and create a connection with the reader. The best A3s are visually appealing and can be understood even by those not familiar with the process or problem in question.
6. Do not prefill sections or work out of sequence. If someone is assigned an A3 and comes up with countermeasures before root cause, coaching on the process is needed!

At this point, start using A3s for two purposes: (a) solving problems in frontline teams and in management, and (b) creating and updating standard work and leader standard work.

Solving Problems

The A3 is your primary tool to teach and reinforce PDCA thinking. Put it into action using the already defined problem identification and escalation process on your visual boards. At the front line, you already have visuals indicating that a problem exists and who is assigned to resolve it. The A3 is a natural next step to facilitate solving the problem. Have the person assigned to the problem go through the A3 process. Name an appropriate sponsor and/or coach that can help the associate learn the process and has the authority to authorize the validated countermeasure to be implemented. Nothing is more disheartening than spending time on the A3 process only to realize a promising countermeasure will not be implemented.

Getting started with A3s is not easy, so anticipate that there will be hiccups along the way and be prepared to step in and assist. Add space on your visual boards to display A3 WIP and completed ones as well. Celebrate when one is finished and publicly praise and recognize those who worked on it. Build excitement around problem solving; making the process fun will reinforce the new philosophy that problems are not bad.

Updates to Standard Work

As you learned in Chapter 5, standard work is core to process improvement as a baseline from which we improve. Unless we stabilize the way work is done and practice a common process, there is no consistent baseline from which to deploy further improvements. But what is the process to improve the standard? A3s provide the answer.

At the end of the day, what we are trying to do is to influence how people perceive their daily work. We want them to see that work has two parts: doing the work and improving the work. When better ways of performing work are discovered through the process of solving problems, it is essential that standard work documents get updated to represent the new, improved way of doing things. Remember the Taichi Ohno[20] quote from Chapter 5: "Where there is no standard, there can be no kaizen."

When an associate has an idea to improve standard work, an A3 should be used to show that the changes have been thoughtfully considered, including any unintended effects on other processes, before the standard is changed. The A3 becomes the currency of process change within the organization. It ensures that process changes are relatively easy to make, while also ensuring that the change does not optimize a local process at the expense of the overall system. Because it drives methodical problem solving and PDCA thinking, A3s act as a governor of sorts, leveling the amount of change to what the organization can absorb at any given time. Using the A3 process for updates to standard work recognizes that process improvement must enable associates and consider the right pace of change for the organization.

Kata

For problem solving to really become embedded into people's daily routines, lean cannot be experienced as additive—just another task piled on to their already overloaded schedule. Your people are already very busy dealing with the work tasks, projects, emergencies, and endless challenges of their jobs. To begin successfully integrating this kind of work, problem solving might be a 5- to 10-minute working discussion, not in the form of a sit-down meeting or a long, drawn out analysis. It becomes a key element of our daily work as we change the way we think about doing our work and improving the way we do our work. Problem solving is the heart of improving our work. You problem solve in very short cycles so that you can check and adjust often because it is during the check/adjust phases that most of the deep learning takes place.[21] The trick is to embed problem solving as a *normal* part of the work routine rather than a separate activity.

We use the word *routine* in describing what needs to become a repetitive pattern of behavior as to how we address problems. Another word for a practiced routine is kata.[22] In his landmark book, *Toyota Kata*[7], Mike Rother uses the term to capture the underlying thought patterns practiced at Toyota in its approach to problem solving and application of the lean tools and methods. As Rother points out with the familiar maxim, "All models are wrong, but some are useful."[23] PDCA is a useful model! It turns out that as we begin to get better at lean problem solving (what Rother calls the improvement kata or IK), we also get better at effectively applying other lean tools (like A3, visual management, and standard work). We get better because we think more clearly and more deliberately. Problem solving is not *extra* work; rather, it is *the* work!

There is a widespread misconception that kata is simply another rendering of PDCA, and on the surface it may appear that way. But if you look deeper (and begin to practice), the improvement kata provides an amazingly effective mechanism to strengthen what is often the weakest part of most people's A3s: the analysis and proposed countermeasures sections. Although the questions appear to be simple, when used with an experienced coach, they are incredibly effective at assisting people to acknowledge what they know, how they know it, and what they need to know to get closer to truly understanding cause and effect. The more clearly we understand cause and effect, the more discerning our proposed countermeasures, and the more profound our learning is as we test them!

The improvement kata is made up of five key questions that the coach asks the learner (the person trying to understand and solve the problem). These questions may seem simple, but they are extremely powerful in supporting people to expand and deepen the way they think about dealing with problems and making improvements:

1. What is the target condition?
2. What is the actual condition right now?
3. What obstacles are now preventing you from reaching the target condition? Which *one* are you addressing now?
4. What is your next step/PDCA experiment?
5. How quickly can we *go and see* what you have learned?

The coaching kata (CK) is focused on managing the learner's experience practicing problem solving. In order to be a good coach, you need to be able to perform lean problem solving skillfully following an established framework and you have to be able to teach it. Good coaching is all about guiding people to discover things on their own rather than directing them to take specific actions. Stéphane Mallarmé[24] said, "To define is to kill. To suggest is to create." A key coaching skill (worth mentioning again) is to ask questions to lead the learner to discover something new without stealing the learning experience from the learner (by telling him or her). Dave Verble[26] describes this as coaching for development versus coaching for correction.

Effective coaching is a one-on-one activity because the coach and the learner need to connect at a very personal level in order to develop the trust and mutual respect required for effective learning to take place (once again, respect plays a central role in the improvement process!). Three keys to good coaching include (a) following a set routine, (b) asking open-ended questions, and (c) listening deeply with the intent to see the issue through the other person's eyes. (Ask yourself, "Where is the learner in his understanding?") This third element is particularly challenging and requires humility on the part of the coach.

People and teams using a problem-solving routine learn as they attempt to reach new levels of performance and, most importantly, adjust based on what they learn in the process of trying to make things better. The kata community has exploded since *Toyota Kata* was first published in 2009. We encourage you to check out the resources made available at the *Toyota Kata* website.[26]

Why Thinking Is Less Important Than Behavior!

It may seem funny that we end a chapter on problem solving with a statement like this! While it is important to understand lean problem solving intellectually, comprehension is not the key to becoming a good problem solver. *The key to becoming a good problem solver is to practice being a good problem solver.* In order to learn, we must experience firsthand the impact of acting differently.

The most effective practice is using the PDCA learning cycle in your work at your gemba—as a part of your daily routine! The more you integrate active learning (aka problem solving) into your daily routine, the more proficient at structured problem solving you will become. The more frequently you indulge your brain in structured thinking about problems, the sooner you'll create reliable mental habits to think about, understand, and solve problems! When the consequences of our actions create better results, we learn by doing and shift our habits to new ways of acting and thinking.

Notes

1. The Shingo Institute is a nonprofit organization whose mission is to guide leaders in creating sustainable, principle-based cultures of excellence. http://www.shingoprize.org.
2. Brian Hinken, *Confessions of a Recovering Knower,* The Systems Thinker, September 2005, p. 2.
3. For a great discussion on this topic, pick up Carol Dweck, *Mindset: The New Psychology of Success* (Random House, 2006).
4. Non-value-added activities include actions that add cost and take time but do not create value. These include rework, overprocessing, creating defects, waiting, movement, transportation, partially completed work, multitasking, overcomplexity, overengineering, poor inputs and materials, excessive handoffs, building technical debt, unused employee creativity, etc.
5. If we truly understand the reasons why an outcome is happening, then it's not an issue that requires structured problem solving; we just need to attack the cause. If we can't effectively address the cause, then *that* becomes our problem!
6. Perhaps the quintessential learning organization is Toyota. Toyota is by no means perfect, but what it does perhaps better than any other company is learn and adjust to changing conditions. This is notable considering their performance after the massive recalls of 2010 related to unintended acceleration. The popular press was quick to announce the fall of mighty Toyota, but the news was a bit premature. Toyota has once again climbed back on top of the vehicle dependability rankings with the Lexus brand and notably the Camry in the midsize category (JD Power 2014 Vehicle Dependability Study). The point is not that mistakes and problems don't occur; the point is how you react when they do.
7. If you haven't read Mike Rother, *Toyota Kata* (McGraw–Hill, 2009), you need to.
8. Mike is a certified yoga instructor and borrowed this practice from over 20 years of yoga and meditation practice.
9. The scientific method is based on identifying a hypothesis (theory), developing an experiment, and proving or disproving it based on the experiment's empirical results. A foundation of modern science, the scientific method is methodical, meticulous, structured, and rigorous.
10. The electric light bulb had been invented 50 years earlier; Edison's goal was to find a suitable filament to make the incandescent electric light a viable device.
11. PDCA (Plan–Do–Check–Adjust) is also described as PDSA (Plan–Do–Study–Act), 1936. The evolution of the problem-solving cycle dates back to the 1930s and Graduate School of the Department of Agriculture Washington, D.C., 1936 (Washington, DC: Graduate School of the Department of Agriculture). http://www.cologic.nu/files/evolution_of_the_pdsa_cycle.pdf.

12. This is a meta-improvement process in the sense that we ask ourselves, "How can we improve our improvement methodology?"
13. Read how Toyota describes its production system at http://www.toyota.com .au/toyota/company/operations/toyota-production-system.
14. For a great look into the impact of bias, see Howard J. Ross, *Everyday Bias: Identifying and Navigating Unconscious Judgments in Our Daily Lives* (Rowman & Littlefield, 2014).
15. The scientific method comprises the principles and empirical processes of discovery and demonstration considered characteristic of or necessary for scientific investigation, generally involving the observation of phenomena, the formulation of a hypothesis concerning the phenomena, experimentation to demonstrate the truth or falseness of the hypothesis, and a conclusion that validates or modifies the hypothesis. http://www.thefreedictionary.com /Scientific+thinking.
16. Here is a great source: http://www.lean.org/common/display/?o=1314.
17. For a detailed description of the A3 process along with examples and coaching advice, see John Shook's book *Managing to Learn* (Lean Enterprise Institute, 2008), a must-read for every lean manager.
18. A Pareto chart is a bar graph sorted in descending order to show which issues are the major contributors to specific conditions. Associated with the 80/20 rule, Pareto analysis shows which inputs have the greatest impact on the outcome.
19. Get rid of language like, "If this is such a problem, why haven't you fixed it already?"
20. Taichi Ohno, Executive VP at Toyota, is credited as the person who did the most to structure the Toyota Production System as an integrated framework.
21. Special thanks to John Shook, Chairman and CEO of the Lean Enterprise Institute, for sharing this insight.
22. A kata is a system of training exercises for practitioners of the martial arts (think Karate Kid!). The word literally means model or pattern.
23. This quote is attributed to statistician George Box (1919–2013).
24. Stéphane Mallarmé (1842–1898) was a French poet and author.
25. David Verble worked with Toyota as manager of Human Resource Development for North America, is a member of the Lean Enterprise Institute faculty, and coauthor of the book *Perfecting Patient Journeys* (Lean Enterprise Institute, 2012).
26. http://www-personal.umich.edu/~mrother/Homepage.html.

Chapter 7

Everything Is Visible

A picture is worth a thousand words.

Introduction

We've all heard the famous saying that opens this chapter, and intuitively we know that it's true. Seeing a picture of a favorite memory, a beautiful vacation spot, or a tragedy evokes feelings inexpressible in words. Pictures instantly convey information and draw us into the story being told. Somehow, this knowledge has not been translated into our workplaces. Data are often hidden in words and spreadsheets and reports. Vital information is obscured from those that need it most, resulting in poor decision making, missed opportunities, and disengagement. If a picture is worth a thousand words, information made visible in the workplace is priceless.

Making the Invisible Visible

Visuality is a great word to represent a lean organization. Visuality is the state of being visible, and that is what lean is really all about, right? Seeing waste, seeing the potential in associates, seeing value flow through the company to the customer—all worthy components of the lean enterprise. But why is it so important to make things visible in our organizations?

Visual management allows us to represent in the physical workplace that which is not visible on its own. The flow of information, the status of a work item, the satisfaction of the customer, the quality of our software, and so on can be made visible. Revealing these invisible things allows us to manage them, to improve them, and to ensure that the value we provide to all stakeholders is at its maximum. Visual management allows us to quickly identify abnormal conditions, create common understanding and context, drive accountability, and increase communication and collaboration. It gives us *compelling evidence that everything is right* rather than having to guess if something is wrong.

At every step of the transformation you will encounter *visual resisters*—those who will attempt to prevent the display of information at your company. Some are misguided but well intentioned, perhaps the HR staffer protecting personal information or the facilities supervisor trying to keep the walls looking pristine. Others—especially some of our IT peers—are not as benevolent and will fight against the very idea of visuality. You are transforming IT after all! Our natural inclination as technologists is to apply technology to all things. Why go through the trouble of manually updating visuals (gasp!) when we can automate, digitize, and produce slick reports? Time and again in organizations, we have seen well-meaning people sabotaging the lean transformation by hiding the very information that needs to be made accessible to all.

The Visual Journey

From this point forward, make the commitment: *If it's important to the organization, it will be made visible.* Strategy, process, quality, delivery, staffing, successes, and problems—everything; bring a level of transparency and trust to your company that can only exist in the visual workplace. In *Visual Thinking, Visual Workplace*, Gwendolyn Galsworth summarizes this well: "A visual workplace is a self-ordering, self-explaining, self-regulating, and self-improving work environment—where what is supposed to happen does happen, on time, every time, day or night—because of visual solutions."[1] Any company that makes the commitment to unlocking hidden data needed by its workforce out of spreadsheets and reports will have an inherent advantage over the competition because we can only improve what we can see and understand.

Lean Visual Management

Why is visual management so important for a lean transformation? Implementing a visual organization will fast-track your transformation by

1. Creating a shared understanding of the current situation and where we want to go in the future
2. Drawing leadership to the gemba, where the real work happens
3. Driving accountability and continuous improvement

Creating a Common Understanding

One of the biggest problems in IT is the lack of transparency. How many times have you encountered a situation where it seems everyone on the project has a different perception of what is actually going on? The project manager is managing to a plan that's very precise, but that everyone else on the team knows is not realistic. The development team is going along with the cost estimate knowing full well there's no credible chance they can complete the project with the funding provided. The testing team thinks the developers are *literally* smoking crack before coding; the developers think it's the testers doing the smoking. The customers have their fingers crossed hoping for the best because they have no idea of what's really going on, except that IT *never* seems to be right about the schedule or cost. And all of the dependent teams are playing *launch chicken*, waiting for another team to blink first and say they can't make the release date so that the blame for the miss is not on them! Sound familiar?

What if we could ensure that—for better or worse—everyone had the same understanding of the current actual conditions; you'd be on board, right? Visual management systems solve these problems by creating readily available data about the execution of the work of IT. The data enable people to engage in the work and develop shared understanding and insight. Visuals are displayed close to where the work is happening and where the people that need the insight can see them. This applies not just to work in process but also to the strategy of the organization, a topic covered in Chapter 10, "The Importance of Strategic Alignment."

Drawing Leadership to the Gemba

Lean leaders have a direct connection to their associates and the work they deliver every day. In fact, the primary source of engagement for associates is their relationship with their direct manager.[2] The manager plays the role of coach, teaching problem solving and developing each associate to his or her full potential. The connection is important for executives as well. We often see executives that are removed from the realities of daily work life and whose understanding of how strategy is being mobilized is based on fantasy. Connection to the day-to-day work, successes and failures, is critical in setting and executing strategic direction and vision.

Without visuals, both management and leadership at the front line are working in the dark, and it is nearly impossible to work effectively. Lean expounds that the management team be at the gemba regularly, but without visuals, how could they possibly understand what is going on? Visuals at the gemba make it easy for managers and executives to engage the people at their work. Without visuals, discussions between managers and associates are less about meaningful dialogue and feel more like interrogations. When leaders don't know what is going on, they cannot effectively lead or support their people.

An effective visual management system draws leaders closer to value-added work on a regular cadence. For senior executives this might be reviewing the visuals of the next two layers down in the organization every week and frontline visuals once a month. The visual system is supported through regular reviews at intervals defined in leader standard work (more on this topic in Chapter 9).

Driving Accountability and Continuous Improvement

Oftentimes in our workplaces we don't really know who is supposed to do what and when it is supposed to happen. How many times has a deadline been missed or a defect released into a production environment simply due to a lack of communication or awareness by someone who needed to know? If your company is like most, more times than you can count. Making your processes visible, making commitments visible, and having real conversations about the issues of the day drive collaboration and accountability. Contrary to popular opinion, very few people arrive at work each day wondering how they can screw something up! We know it feels like it sometimes, but everyone else is *not* trying to make your life difficult! Most people want to do good work, collaborate, and help others. It's the lack of a comprehensive system that provides needed information that gets in the way. Putting tasks on a project plan or in a report rarely moves people to action and keeps them aligned in a way that a well-placed, up-to-date visual system does.

When everyone has a common understanding of what is supposed to happen, there is a much better chance that it actually will happen. It's one thing to miss a deadline in some project manager's plan; it is wholly another matter when you miss a deadline that is posted for everyone to see (and that you have committed to in a standup meeting).[3] In Chapter 9 we'll discuss the use of a tiered system to drive further accountability within the management team. Creating an interlocking, tiered visual management system with line-of-sight metrics provides a fail-safe way to ensure that all areas of the organization are aligned to purpose or True North.

Everyone in the lean organization has an additional responsibility: continuous improvement. We discussed earlier in this book that it's not just people's job to *do their job*, but rather to find better ways to do their jobs. Making continuous improvement visible—showing the progress the group is making on solving problems, process improvement, and delivery—ensures that it stays a priority for the company.

Expanding the Model Line Visual Management System

You should already have elements of a visual system in place, created during the transformation startup. Notably, visual boards for the management team focused on status, process improvement, and True North; frontline boards focused on work-in-process and problems should also be in place. Let's take a look at how to expand the system to create even more of an impact.

Walk before You Run

The first step of expanding the system further is to take time to reflect on the current state of the visuals you already have in place. Are they being used and kept up to date every day? Do they drive better decision making? Closer collaboration? Or have they become glorified wallpaper, ignored except when the team is pressed to use them? Visual displays are only as good as the value they provide to the organization. A stale visual system does more harm than good, becoming a running joke in the organization and empowering people to disengage from the transformation. Commit to implement only what can be sustained in the organization. If your visuals are not being used, take the time now to understand why and check/adjust before proceeding.

"Uncommon" Visual Management

Lean IT visual systems are a balancing act of what's needed by and easiest to use for the team that owns particular visual boards, and what others outside the direct team need to know. Often there is a core set of people that will use a particular visual very frequently in order to get their daily work done, while there is another set of stakeholders who need information from the board as well, but less frequently. There is sometimes tension between these groups as to how the data will be represented. The team that creates and maintains the boards has intimate knowledge of their work and may want to use shortcuts, acronyms, and other codified language unfamiliar to those outside the team. The outsiders, who include managers, other teams, or customers, want easy-to-understand data that don't require a special decoder ring—which unfortunately means extra work for the team to create and maintain the boards.

There is a need for visual systems to be understood without specialized team knowledge. Creating visuals that only a select group of people can understand—when others outside the team need the information too—is just as bad as hiding it in a report. The point of a visual system is to radiate information; requiring someone from the team to act as an interpreter not only defeats the purpose, but it also wastes time. If information needs to be known, it should be visible and accessible without needing a translator.

But not all information made visible is needed by outsiders. Some of the visuals are only needed by a specific team or group of people. For example, for a team that has created *rules* for how members should act in the team space, the rules are likely only needed by the team. In this case, don't micromanage the look and feel; leave it up to the team. Another example would be when the work flow of a team that interacts with five other teams needs to be understood by members of the other teams and perhaps project managers as well. When visual information is needed by both the team and outsiders, what is the right balance between team efficiency and outsider understanding?

To answer this question, many companies require some level of standardization for their visuals. This allows people in disparate areas the ability to understand the visuals of another group quickly while not placing too high a burden on the team that maintains the visual system. Similarly to standard work, in this case standardization means a baseline put in place because it's the best way we know how to do something right now but it may change in the future. Be careful not to resort to something we call *commonization*.

Commonization is doing something the same way for the purpose of consistency. Consistency is not the purpose of a lean visual management system; providing visuals that drive collaboration, understanding, and accountability, and that act as a magnet to draw people in is the purpose. In some cases that requires standardization. The standards can be as simple as posting a key for the colors or codes used, or as elaborate as an integrated numbering system to be used for all work flow items. Each transformation is unique and there will be some trial and error as you work to find the right balance for your company.[4]

Additional Visual Elements for the Model Line

Understanding the theory behind visual management is well and good, but what are the next steps for your transformation? There is good news and bad news. The good news is that there are a few more elements of the visual system outlined in this chapter for you to implement. The bad news is that they are not enough. Unfortunately, there is no one right way to complete a visual management system. In fact, your system will never be complete. The visuals are subject to a never-ending cycle of continuous improvement, just like all the other tools and practices in your lean system. Get used to this cycle! As a lean leader your mind becomes restless, looking for ways to improve, eliminate waste, and engage associates. The best lean leaders develop *kaizen eyes*—always on the lookout for daily process improvement opportunities.

For now, let's take a look at some new elements to add to the visual management system.

Problem Solving

The first additional element to add to both the management and frontline systems is making visible your A3 process. In Chapter 6 we discussed using the A3 for problem solving and updates to standard work. Previously we created a visual to represent problems on our boards; the A3 now gives us a methodical, scientific method to approach solving those problems. It is just as important to show the progress of the countermeasures addressing identified problems as it is to show the problems themselves. Making visible the progress reinforces a culture of accountability that, when a problem arises, the company takes it seriously and empowers associates to work toward a fix. Associates see that what matters to them matters to management and gradually become more comfortable making problems known to all. If problems go up on the board, but nothing ever happens, it reinforces a culture that the problems of associates don't matter to the management team and that we accept them as permanent conditions. Making the A3 process visible breaks that cycle. If you haven't already, expand the problem-solving section of your boards to allow for the display of A3s—both work-in-process and completed. See Figure 7.1 for an example of an A3 board that is easy to implement.

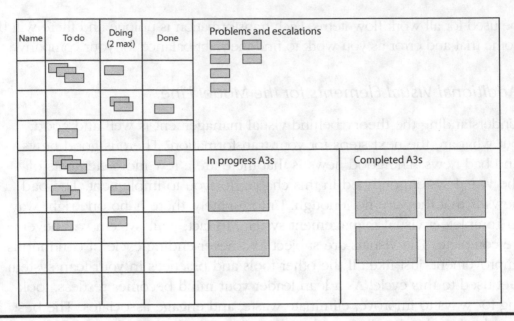

Figure 7.1   Visually representing A3s demonstrates the organization's commitment to problem solving and continuous improvement.

Even if your organization is not using the A3 process, or is but uses other methods as well, represent your problems visually. Whether or not you are using A3s, the key is to make scientific problem solving visible within the organization. When there is a problem, demonstrate visually the actions and discoveries that are happening in response. The impact of this powerful practice drives new behaviors from your people.

Focus visuals not only on the problems of the associates, but also on the problems encountered by the management team. Make sure the visuals for the management team are also updated to display problems and A3s. The best way to ensure that associates are focused on actively using the A3 process is to see the behavior demonstrated by the management team. If you want the staff to stop solution jumping and use PDCA, start with yourself and the full management team. As with all the lean tools, the management team must take accountability to lead the way in both word and behavior.

Process Changes and Continuous Improvement

Outlined in Chapter 6, the A3 is a great way to make changes to standard work and reinforce PDCA thinking. These standard work updates should be made visible as well. The reason is twofold: (1) you want to ensure that those impacted by the transformation see that regularly occurring process improvement is an expectation, not just a seemingly random occurrence, and (2) visibly representing process change as it is happening gives more staff a chance to weigh in on the issue. If the A3 owner has lived the principles of PDCA, he or she will have already involved those that participate in the standard work process being addressed in the creation of the A3. If it is a complete surprise, however, perhaps the owner needs some coaching on the A3 process and collaboration. The visual display of process improvement acts as a poka yoke[5] to ensure that the right people have been involved.

Ideas, Suggestions, and Observations

Consider adding a place in the visual management system for continuous improvement suggestions as well. To this point in your transformation, the focus has been on problem solving and changes to established processes. Now is the time to add an area for organic improvement ideas as well. This is a spot for the imaginative and innovative suggestions of your workforce to be showcased and assessed for experimentation. Making improvement suggestions visible creates accountability that the ideas will be addressed and provides an easy mechanism to harvest the innovation potential within each associate. Create a place for suggestions and observations[6] on the boards of both the frontline and management teams.

Not all of the ideas will be a home run or even something that is viable to implement. However, making continuous improvement ideas visible helps ensure that they will have a final disposition, and that the submitter knows what became of his suggestion. Nothing is more frustrating than the infamous *suggestion box* that never amounts to any change, and nothing is more harmful than ignoring the ideas of your people! The visuality ensures that each idea is evaluated and *something* happens to it. And it makes certain that that something is visible for all to see. Caution: ensure that you have thought this through and are prepared for the initial flood of ideas and observations that often surface, or you will have some major damage control to deal with![7]

Recognition

Recognition is a fundamental element of an associate's work experience. Research has shown in numerous studies that associates are more engaged when their manager regularly recognizes their work.[8] It's common sense really: Everyone wants to feel appreciated and valued. But while everyone

CASE STUDY: THE IMPROVEMENT BOARD THAT DIDN'T DRIVE IMPROVEMENT

Mike worked with a client who was keen to use visual management to focus associates on the highest priority work, drive improvement, and create involvement by leadership. The client aggressively put up *Improvement Boards* throughout the entire organization using a standard layout that included space for daily work focus, roadblocks and escalations, and process improvement. But after 60 days it was clear that no one was using the system to drive improvement. The client had failed to recognize that creating visual boards was necessary but not sufficient. It was also necessary to change daily behavior to leverage the intent of all sections of the board, which included process improvement.

To make process improvement part of daily discussions, the client began to address the problem when managers and leaders noticed the blank spaces on the boards. Once the issue was identified, countermeasures and coaching were put into place to support new behaviors and team dialogue that balanced the problem du jour with critical improvements that were vital to the company. Without a simple, visual, in-your-face indication that something was wrong, we suspect the situation would have continued indefinitely.

Keep in mind that the visual management system has a dual purpose: make the work visible *and* keep improvement a central part of the daily discussion.

knows this intuitively, in practice, recognition often goes unspoken. An easy fix to this problem is to make recognition visible and a part of your standups. Create a section on your visual boards where anyone can recognize anyone else for a job well done. Post positive comments received from customers and co-workers. Publicly praise individuals when appropriate and take accountability to ensure that regular updates occur. Create an entry in every manager's leader standard work to ensure that this remains a focus for the organization.

Standard Work for Visual Management

We have said it before: The only thing worse than no visual management is visual management that is never updated. Without relevant data with regular updates, the visual system decays and is rightfully ignored. If the visual system becomes stale, no one will use it. If no one uses it, it becomes harder to get people to update it. You get the point: Visual systems require a routine of regular maintenance. The lean visual system should become the primary way to obtain needed information in your company. To do that you need a disciplined process to ensure that updates to the visuals happen on time, every time. And you need clear definitions of who is responsible for the updates and when they should occur. To ensure that updates to visuals occur and the *who* and *when* are clear, let's modify standard work.

Define in standard work the process of keeping the visuals up to date. You can also build the standard work directly into the visual system and visually list who updates each section of the boards and when that update occurs. You can add features on the boards such as a *last-updated indicator* or *updated by* as your situation dictates as well.

Distributed Teams and Visual Management

In the text so far, the focus has primarily been on co-located teams. For the model line transformation, we recommended earlier to use a group that resides in the same location. It is much easier to guide your first lean transformation when everyone is in the same setting than to deal with multiple locations, time zones, cultural norms, etc. This approach also allows you to practice using lean tools and principles to radically change the way the group operates. You are not simply implementing some techniques and running a training class; you are also fundamentally altering the way work gets done. Implementing tools and techniques is the easy part. The hard part is changing the collective mindset of the group to affect lasting cultural change. Adding in the complexity of a distributed workforce from day one increases complexity and might be too much to ask.

However, this may not be your reality. You may be dealing with off-shore development, a data center in a different building from your primary group, or a virtual workplace. You are probably wondering if visual management still applies. It does, but this requires some creativity and flexibility.

We have found that visual management is most effective when it can be viewed in its original form by everyone on the team and cannot be *turned off.* By this we mean it is physically in the workspace—not on a monitor, not in a report, not on a Sharepoint site. Electronic forms of visual management can be turned off at any time and easily ignored. But a physical board smacks you in the face every time you walk by it saying, "Look at me." So what can be done to mimic this in a distributed world?

If your situation is just a few remote locations, simply replicate the visuals in those locations. This can be done using low-cost labor such as interns or entry-level staff whose standard work includes keeping the visual system in sync. Any place where you have multiple team members in different locations, try this approach. At the time of this writing there are also a number of promising electronic physical boards that can stay in sync across geographic distance with near instantaneous updates. They are only promising at this point because they currently do not offer the flexibility of a physical board created with markers, tape, magnets, and cards, but the technology is rapidly closing the gap and it is worth keeping an eye on them for the future.

If you have a lone wolf or two on the team, a different approach is required. In this situation try low-cost/low-effort solutions first. Before the standup each day, send a high-resolution picture of the boards to the team member so that he or she can use it as his or her own personal visual board for the standup and work of the day. Create a process whereby this team member's updates make it to the board in real time. A handheld USB web cam works as well in many cases. Other, more expensive options include investing in video conferencing or telepresence technologies that emulate the in-person experience, but so far these are not particularly effective. With a little creativity you can bring distributed team members into the collaborative workspace you are creating.

Don't let the current situation of a geographically dispersed team hold you back from implementing lean. You are only limited by your imagination in applying the tools and principles in this situation. Over the long term you should evaluate the relative benefits you get from a separated team that collaborates virtually versus the benefits of a co-located team.

Visual Management Wrap-Up

Visuality is one of the most important tools in your lean toolkit. The behaviors that it reinforces—accountability, going to the gemba, communication, and collaboration—are foundational to a successful lean transformation. Taking the time to build a robust visual system along with the appropriate processes to maintain it will provide incredible benefits to your first lean journey and deliver a basis from which to expand to other areas of the company.

Notes

1. Gwendolyn D. Galsworth, *Visual Workplace, Visual Thinking* (Portland, OR: Visual-Lean Enterprise Press, 2005), p. 23.
2. https://www.q12.gallup.com/Public/en-us/Kits.
3. Ensure that the responsible party for the work has made the commitment. Simply putting up unrealistic commitments for people without their buy-in is not lean visual management.
4. Much credit for the concept and topic of avoiding commonization in this chapter goes to two individuals: David Mann, author of *Creating a Lean Culture*, 3rd edition (Taylor & Francis, 2015) and the gemba trips and conversations he had with Tom and the rest of the management team about Nationwide IT's transformation of the Application Development Center; and R. Gary Butler, Executive-in-Residence, Fisher College of Business.
5. Poka yoke commonly means *mistake proofing*. The term is used extensively in lean manufacturing for things like devices or instruments that prevent defects from occurring. But the term can also be applied to other functions, like IT. In this case we are using a visual poka yoke to ensure that collaboration and inspection occur before a process is changed to ensure that the change has been thought through from a variety of perspectives.
6. It is important to make sure that people understand that they do not need to have a *solution* in order to make a suggestion or an observation.
7. Mike made this mistake as a plant manager many years ago. He asked for suggestions and made promises that all suggestions would receive a response in 48 hours. Unfortunately, the infrastructure was not in place nor were all the managers prepared to fulfill this commitment. Visual management makes mistakes vividly clear to all as well!
8. While there are many studies on the impact of recognition on the work life of employees, we'd recommend the research done by the Gallup organization and their "Gallup Q[12]."

Chapter 8

Why Management (Still) Matters

Right now, your company has 21st-century Internet-enabled business processes, mid-20th-century management processes, all built atop 19th-century management principles.

Gary Hamel[1]
The Future of Management, 2007

Introduction

With the advent of agile, many in the IT community have adopted a *no managers needed here* philosophy.[2] While self-directed development teams have certainly shifted the role of managers, we believe very strongly that managers are an essential key to enabling and sustaining positive change in IT. Great managers provide the support needed to nurture people development, both technically and socially, as well as creating a culture of transparency. Often it is managers (and no one else) who effectively navigate upstream and downstream channels of collaboration to coordinate work inputs and outcomes into the hands of end users and customers.

Lost in Translation

In Chapter 3, we explored the importance of purpose and the significance of getting people aligned to a common goal. Sounds easy but the tricky part is getting people to see and embrace how company purpose and strategy directly apply to their daily work. High-level objectives such as Google's "Don't Be Evil"[3] motto may be difficult to translate into daily tactics. People are right to ask, "What does that look like?"

It is the managers in your organization who play a pivotal role in making a vivid connection between purpose and behavior—connecting strategy to execution. They are perfectly positioned to decipher your company's intention, objectives, and strategy from high-level aspirations to specific actions. It is useful to think of your organization as being composed of three levels: associates, managers, and leaders. The associates include everyone at the front line creating the services, products, and information customers consume. Managers are those people who are responsible for the performance of others—this includes team leads, supervisors, managers, directors, and VPs. Executive leaders are the ones who set the strategic direction of your company and are held responsible for overall performance. In a lean IT transformation, it is imperative that we are clear on what the primary focus of each role should be. See Table 8.1.

For an organization to be effective, people in all three roles need to do their jobs very well. Unfortunately, there is often a lack of clarity on *what* the job entails. We all know managers that seem to think their job is primarily about control—directing people as to what actions to take and what not

Table 8.1 Roles, Primary Responsibility, and Focus

Role	Primary Responsibility	Focus
Associates	Frontline workers creating value for external and internal customers	Do the work; improve the way we work
Managers	The performance of people (divisions, departments, teams)	Develop your people; get results; sustain improvements
Leaders	The overall performance of the organization	Create and articulate the vision; set strategic direction; develop your people; achieve sustained results

to do. We've worked with companies where the associates don't know what the CEO looks like or have never seen the general manager of their division. It's not uncommon that associates don't really know the other members of their workgroup, let alone the people who supply them work inputs or those who receive their work. It's as though people are living in a bubble, seeing their job as isolated from the work of others! With such a limited view and circle of communication, it's no wonder we possess differing ideas on roles and responsibilities.

You're Only as Good as the People around You

Another critical role of managers, particularly in support of a lean IT trans-formation, is developing people. This is a skill set many managers lack when the emphasis of the company is primarily on *results* and people development is given lip service and effectively downgraded to a low priority. Just as concerning, it is often viewed as nothing more than occa-sional training in technical skills. The people development we are talking about here refers to problem solving, communication, and teamwork skills. Problem solving is as much of a mindset as it is a skill set and learning a new skill often requires a competent guide or coach. We'll discuss coaching later in this chapter.

Managers are those who are responsible for the performance of oth-ers. If they actively work with their people and go to the gemba regu-larly, they begin to understand and appreciate the power of people armed with problem solving skills working in highly effective teams. Unfortunately, many work environments still live by the leader–follower model,[4] with a prevailing culture where managers do the thinking and associates do what they are told. When people are asked, "Can you tell me what you do here?" we are amazed at how many IT professionals respond, "Whatever my boss tells me to do!" This response is clearly an outdated twentieth century paradigm and may indicate that management is not being encouraged, measured, or supported to actively develop people.

Your Managers Are the Key

As we mentioned earlier, there are managers who do not lead and leaders who fail to manage. Stephen Covey said, "You manage things, and you lead people."[5] We agree, but we also feel the word *manage* is so widely used throughout our society that we need to better define and apply it to reinforce the change we want to see in our organization. Excluding the term from our vocabulary is not going to make things better.

Most of us have had a direct experience with a manager who attempted to control our thoughts and behaviors. This is the legacy of Taylorism,[6] the scientific management approach from the early 1900s that powered the Industrial Revolution. Taylor believed people needed to be controlled and directed to *extract* value from them. The implicit assumption is that people are lazy, undisciplined, and aimless. Without direct top-down control by management, they will not do the right things or be productive. Focused on efficiency and economies of scale, this view of people as mindless workers led to robust control-based systems of centralized decision making and enforcement hierarchies. Taylor's Industrial Age paradigm influences our workplaces to this very day.

Now roll the tape forward roughly 100 years. Today, some managers have evolved to move away from coercive command-and-control management styles to more inclusive, participative approaches. As stress levels increase, it seems that most regress to directive command management, which indicates that this pattern of management runs deep within our basic emotional predispositions. In a lean transformation, managers play a key role, especially if previous programs, initiatives, and promises that have since been abandoned have damaged the trust of your people. It is the managers that will demonstrate that lean is not another flavor-of-the-month program, but rather a new way of doing business, of showing up, and of being.

Starting your transformation with the associates but without the full support, participation, and understanding of the managers won't work because people focus on the things their boss talks about most often. The associates are busy doing the work necessary to create value for your customers. It is your managers who should be providing *both* the technical backing (how to develop needed job skills, *not* specifically how to achieve targeted outcomes) and people development support (how to improve work processes) as they nurture and develop their teams—one person at a time.

To be effective, managers must support the development of people (through problem solving, teamwork, and communication skills) along with technical support on how to do the work. This ideal state, where managers have both technical and social coaching skills, is rare. With the complexity of IT disciplines, managers do not always possess the knowledge to support the vast array of skills their team might have or require. In these cases, the role of a manager is to enable the means to obtain that knowledge. Let's take a look at some of the critical skills necessary to be a lean manager.

Being an Effective Coach

A great manager places the development of people *ahead* of results, knowing that the inevitable outcome of engaged and skilled people is great results. For years, we've been told that managers need to coach, but we have often failed to provide managers with the training and coaching they need to become effective coaches. Many books have been written on the subject of effective coaching, but we'd like to highlight the key essential skills you'll need to drive great behavior and the subsequent results.

Listening

Engaged listening shows respect toward others by demonstrating that their opinions matter. Listening is an essential skill that most of us do miserably. Instead of deeply listening, we formulate what we are going to say next, think about a different topic, don't listen at all, or multitask with our smartphones—you get the picture. We are not present and in the moment with the other person. Most of us actively filter what is being said,[7] hearing and evaluating only a portion of what the other person is saying. We then base our response exclusively on the information we allowed to enter our awareness, rather than the entire explanation. Considering how important effective communication is and given our poor listening skills, it's amazing we get anything accomplished! We'll have more to say on this important skill later in this chapter.

Communicating

Given our poor listening skills, communication is often a one-way flow of information. To be an effective coach, you need the ability to create a dialogue, an effective conversation where information is flowing between people, not at them! Being a good communicator requires all other coaching skills that work synergistically to create a personal connection between coach and learner. As you begin to develop your listening skills, you'll be amazed at the improvement in your overall communication. Always remember: "Seek first to understand, then to be understood."[8]

Observation

Most people are moving so fast that they miss seeing what is happening around them. We've all had experiences where we failed to hear what was being said and did not see what was happening in front of us. Our fast-paced world of 24/7 news, social media, smartphones, and connectivity only adds to our inability to focus and deeply observe our environment.[9] We'll cover Go and See in a few pages and explore the importance of this coaching skill.

Support

As a manager, supporting your people is part of your job. But what does it mean to effectively support someone? In a lean IT transformation, it includes connecting with a person at his or her level and providing the nurturing and grooming the person needs to grow professionally as an effective team member. It also includes challenging people to strive toward a worthy goal, which may very likely appear to be out of reach. This is tough work because most people don't get excited (at least at first) about striving for goals that appear to be impossible to achieve. Helping people see the next step is often all it takes to motivate them to take action. As a coach, you must find a balance between challenging and supporting what works best for the person you are working with. One size does not fit all and each member of your team will require a different mix depending on personality, skill level, and willingness to follow an unmarked path of experimentation and problem solving.

Patience

Patience pays; to be a great coach you must demonstrate patience in order to make the necessary space for people to grow. If your people feel pressured and stressed by your impatience, they will take shortcuts and say the things they think you want to hear. This is *fake lean*, imitation learning, and a waste of everyone's time. It turns out that developing your listening skills will also improve your patience, because good listening requires quiet focus. See the simple yet effective listening exercise later in this chapter.

Empowerment

Great coaches possess an ability to share the potential capability they see in someone in such a way that people see it in themselves. People tend to live up to the expectations and perceptions of those they respect and work with. As a coach, your ability to inspire others to see the hidden greatness that lies within them is a necessary talent. Here's a tip: If you can inspire yourself to see *your* potential greatness and use that to drive new behaviors, you will be able to effectively do so with others. Don't get discouraged when you find you are good at this with some people but not with others. This is common and has to do with your natural personality and that of the person you are coaching. You will have an instant connection as a coach with some people, and what feels like a repellent with others. As you gain more experience, you will learn to modify your words and approach to effectively connect with the person you are coaching so they become more self-initiating and empowered. A final note here: Empowerment is not the same thing as "go do whatever you want!" Empowerment is placing people in a position to use their own thoughtful judgment to methodically solve problems. Before you can do this, your team will need the mindset, skill set, and tool set we have been exploring throughout this book.

Respectful Leadership

You can buy people's time and hands with a paycheck, but to access their creative brilliance and deep caring about how to make things better, you must enable and inspire them to see themselves in a much greater role. We have mentioned respect for people several times and now is a good time to dig deeper into this important topic. Most people intuitively understand that getting people to own their problems will lead to higher levels of engagement and drive better problem solving, productivity, quality, teamwork, morale, safety, etc. Here's the key to engaging people: When people know their opinion matters and *accept* ownership of their problems and solutions to those problems, they see themselves as valuable because they feel valued! When they personally align the value-adding elements of their daily work with a motivating purpose, great things begin to happen!

In our experience, the most effective way to enable and inspire people is to connect with them at a very real and personal level. The currency of this connection is respect. Much has been written about respect for people; in fact, it is one of the two main pillars of the Toyota Way, the company's system of values. Toyota describes respect as "… respecting the individuality of each person within the group, respecting their contributions, their ideas, as well as their cultural or personal beliefs. It also means respecting the natural environment."[10] When you connect with people through respect, you instill a yearning to be more and to achieve more.

Leading with Respect

In the book *Lead with Respect*[11], the authors provide some valuable insights on what respect looks like and how respecting people can drive engagement, accountability, hands-on problem solving, and people development. The authors do a skillful job demonstrating lead-with-respect behaviors, exploring seven core components while telling the story of a CEO struggling to create a culture of excellence.

Go and See

This has been a central maxim within lean for many years, but has seldom been practiced by managers. Go and See is all about visiting the gemba to understand by observing—silently watching people and process to *stand in the shoes* of the people doing the work and seeing deeply what their work experience is all about. This seems like an obvious and straightforward thing to do, but it is deceptively difficult for a number of reasons. First of all, most managers are uncomfortable going to the gemba to *just watch* and quickly take charge and tell people what to do. There is certainly a time and place for dialogue with your team, but initially Go and See is about silent observation and learning by looking.

So what are you looking for when you Go and See? First, do your people understand the goals they are trying to achieve? Is it clear whether they are winning (moving closer to their goal) or losing? Next, how well are people working together? What is the degree of collaboration and communication? Finally, how are problems identified, captured, and resolved? Of course, there is more to see and learn, but you need to understand these three areas in order to support your team's success.

Questions to ask as a manager include:

■ Do I Go and See on a routine basis?
■ What is my purpose for visiting the gemba?
■ How much looking and learning do I do (as opposed to talking and directing)?
■ How do I know if my gemba visits are effective?

Challenge

It is important for managers to understand that showing respect to your people is not the same thing as being nice and well mannered. Friendliness and courtesy are not what we are talking about here.[12] To improve performance, people need a challenge—a worthy goal to aspire toward. The more we challenge ourselves and strive to achieve a goal *where we do not know the solution*, the greater our confidence grows as we experience success!

Ballé breaks challenge into four steps:

1. Define success.
2. Agree on the problem(s).
3. Agree on criteria for an acceptable solution.
4. Agree on an acceptable pace of progress.

Questions to ask as a manager include:

- Am I challenging my people to achieve meaningful and specific goals?
- Do team goals align with our organizational purpose?
- Do we have clarity and agreement around the four steps?
- How do I know if my challenge to the team is effective?

Listen

We touched on this key coaching skill earlier in the chapter. Here's a simple exercise you can do to assess your level of listening: The next time you are listening, ask yourself, "Where is my focus right now?"[13] Often the response is a voice in your head that says, "I am thinking about my next meeting" or "I am not entirely focused on what this person is saying." As soon as you notice this, consciously redirect your attention to the speaker's words. If you sense that you missed a significant portion of the conversation, say, "I'm sorry, but I wasn't completely focused. Can you please repeat that last bit?" Of course, don't do this too often or people will stop talking to you!

Questions to ask as a manager include:

- How important is it for me to develop good listening skills?
- What is it like to be standing in the shoes of the other person?

- What are the barriers the other person is facing?
- How would I know if I am accurately seeing things from the other person's perspective?

Teach Problem-Solving Skills

The bonding agent that pulls together the elements of respect for people, organizational purpose, people development, and continuous improvement is problem solving. Problem solving is a universal, topic-neutral mindset, skill set, and tool set that is the centerpiece of leading with respect. If we truly respect people, our most important role as managers is to develop them to their full capabilities. When people feel they have the autonomy, support, and opportunity to improve their work environment, they feel the respect from their managers and peers.

We explore problem solving extensively in Chapter 6 and use the term *problem-solving scientists* to describe the atmosphere of a workplace where methodical problem solving is a way of life. To become good at problem solving, people need

- The opportunity to practice
- Good coaching support
- Time to think
- Time to try things, fail, learn, and try other things

The tragedy we see in the lean community is that many companies only employ event-based, episodic occasions (often referred to as *kaizen events*) to apply problem solving. While periodic problem-solving events can be effective, on their own they are not enough. If you want to effectively instill problem-solving skills in your people, they need to be practicing those skills *every day*. We know this sounds extreme, but we have *never* found a high-performing, lean organization (IT or otherwise) that gained proficiency solely using projects, workshops, and kaizen events to develop these skills.

Questions to ask as a manager include:

- Do I believe that problem solving is a key skill I need to develop in my people?
- Does my team have the opportunity to develop their problem skills every day?

- Am I qualified to coach my team in problem solving?
- If not, what can I do to become a good problem solver myself, and then develop my coaching skills?

Support

As managers, we intuitively know we need to support our teams to achieve the results we are accountable for. In terms of leading with respect, the support we're talking about has everything to do with daily problem solving. As people begin to actively engage in problem solving, they will encounter obstacles to making the changes they want to test, they will experience failures and setbacks, and they will be frustrated and stymied. This is all part of the normal growth process when learning a new skill. Consider the time, effort, and frustration you might have experienced learning to play a new sport (say, golf) or musical instrument. Without some form of nurturing support, you might have given up.

If you think about it, the daily problem solving we're describing is probably radically different from the behavior that you are currently getting from your people. In order for people to want to try new things, they must feel safe and see a potential benefit to making the change. Engaging people with respect to try new things is perhaps the most supportive thing you can do as a manager. Why? Because you want them to do the thinking, the learning, the discovering, and the growing! You cannot do this for them; they *must* do it themselves. Mike likes to say, "Lean is not about trial and error; it's about trial and discovery."

Support your people by encouraging them to proactively take responsibility for solving problems that impact them, trying new ideas, and failing forward[14] by learning from mistakes and tenaciously persevering. Don't allow failures and setbacks to cause you or them to abandon the goal.

Questions to ask as a manager include:

- Do I support my people to become autonomous problem solvers?
- Do I actively encourage them to try new ideas even if they may not work?
- Do I instill a failing-forward mentality in my team?
- What behaviors do I demonstrate when failures and setbacks are encountered?

Enable Teamwork

As a manager who wants to nurture lean thinking and behavior, you very likely know how important effective coordination is within your team and among the various departments and suppliers that provide inputs and receive outputs. Leading with respect includes developing skills to work effectively with others. Communication, including listening, is at the top of our list. If you consider each of the chapters in this book, you may notice that they all contribute to effective collaboration and teamwork: purpose, process, visuality, problem solving, and strategy alignment complement one another to enable effective teamwork.

Comparable to problem solving, effective teamwork requires daily practice to develop the skill set required to be an effective team when things aren't going well and difficulties are encountered. It's easy to be a team when everything is running smoothly, but what happens when a major bug is discovered in a new release? Do we begin pointing figures and deflecting blame, or do we rally as a team to address the issues at hand? It is response to adversity and challenge that defines the degree to which effective teamwork is embedded in the social fabric of a group and of an organization.

Questions to ask as a manager include:

■ How important is effective teamwork? Why?
■ How do I actively encourage (or discourage) effective teamwork with my people?
■ How do I know if my people are effectively working as a team among themselves and with other groups?
■ What happens with my team when difficulties and challenges arise? Do we come together or do we come apart?

Learn

If you want to be a good manager, you need to be curious and always learning from the experiences of gemba. Going to gemba to really see, creating a challenge, deeply listening, teaching problem solving, supporting your people, and enabling effective teamwork will require deep learning on your part. And it never ends! You will be learning, discovering, experimenting, failing, and succeeding for the rest of your career. Learning is *the* skill that will help you to grow as a person and as a manager.

As you learn to apply these skills, you will also discover a deeper understanding of people's potential capabilities as well as your own. Your paradigm of what is achievable will expand, as will your faith in people to accomplish the seemingly impossible. Your understanding of what motivates and inspires people will grow with experience. And perhaps most importantly, your ability to lead with humility will emerge as a part of your character.

Humility, as we are using it here, means that you will be comfortable not having all the answers and value the fact that the answers need to come from the people working for you. The people at the front lines know the problems they face at a level that no manager could ever fully understand. Someone once said, "No idea is held so precious as our own."[15] The people who conceive improvement ideas hold them close, identify with them at a personal level, and commit to making them work.

Lean is about lifelong learning, and leading with respect is perhaps the greatest teacher you can learn from as a manager. It is useful to review these practices on a regular basis (we do it monthly) to reflect on strengths, opportunities, and your next area of personal growth.

The Coach in You—A Reflective Journey

In this chapter we've covered the pivotal role of managers actively engaged as coaches enabling transformation by effectively developing people. Effective coaching drives and accelerates an effective lean IT transformation. The manager's journey is a reflection of the organization's journey. The importance of developing yourself into a great coach can't be overstated, so start now! If you can find a good coach to mentor you, your development will be faster but probably just as painful because of how uncomfortable it feels to step into a new role for which you lack proficiency. As a manager, you may be very comfortable and accustomed to knowing what to do and how to get results. As a coach enabling a lean IT transformation, you may feel woefully inadequate. Relax; this is natural and fundamental to Leading with Respect!

Notes

1. Gary Hamel, *The Future of Management*, Harvard Business Review Press, 2007.
2. See Robert Galen, *We're Going "Agile"… Fire All the Managers!*, May 10, 2014, http://rgalen.com/agile-training-news/2014/4/14/were-going-agile-fire-all-the -managers for a balanced and thoughtful discussion on this topic.

3. Brian Fung, *Google's Search for a Better Motto*, The Washington Post, November 3, 2014, http://www.washingtonpost.com/blogs/the-switch/wp /2014/11/03/larry-page-googles-outgrown-dont-be-evil-and-its-other-mottos/.

4. For an excellent exploration of this concept, see *Turn the Ship Around: A True Story of Turning Followers into Leaders* by L. David Marquet (Penguin Group, 2012).

5. Stephen R. Covey, *Knowledge Workers: 10,000 Times the Productivity*, April 7, 2008, http://www.stephencovey.com.

6. Taylorism is a system of scientific management advocated by Fred W. Taylor. In his view, the task of factory management was to determine the best way for the worker to do the job, to provide the proper tools and training, and to provide incentives for good performance. http://www.britannica.com/EBchecked /topic/1387100/Taylorism

7. This is known as selective listening, a proficiency spouses perfect after many years of marriage!

8. This is the fifth habit in Stephen R. Covey's timeless classic, *The 7 Habits of Highly Effective People* (Simon & Shuster, 1989).

9. For a quick but thorough read on this subject, see *Conquer Cyber Overload—Get More Done, Boost Your Creativity, and Reduce Stress*, by Joanne Cantor, Ph.D. (CyberOutlook Press, 2009).

10. The other pillar is continuous improvement, http://www.toyota.eu/society /Pages/our_people.aspx.

11. Michael and Freddy Ballé, *Lead with Respect: A Novel of Lean Practice* (Lean Enterprise Institute, 2014).

12. We believe that professional courtesy and a smile are essential in creating an effective, comfortable work environment, but these behaviors fall under being a good human being, rather than the respect for people we are describing here.

13. This is a simple adaptation of a mindfulness meditation that Mike has practiced for many years.

14. *Failing forward* is a term made popular by John C. Maxwell in his book of the same name.

15. Mike first heard this described as a fortune cookie quotation discovered by his good friend and colleague, Jake Raymer.

Chapter 9

Sustain Your Progress

It's no use going back to yesterday because I was a different person then.

Lewis Carroll
Alice's Adventures in Wonderland, 1865

Building for the Long Term

By now, you've put in place the vital systems and tools that create a functioning lean IT environment. However, they are not nearly enough to sustain organizational change. Lean systems require constant care and feeding—more so than traditional work systems. Without consistent reinforcement and monitoring, all the hard work you have invested to build the foundational elements of your new system, such as visual management, standard work, and A3 thinking, will lack staying power. Examples abound of lean transformations that were off to a good start but somehow couldn't quite stay the course. In this chapter we'll discuss how to create sustaining actions that will assure that your new lean system operates effectively and continuously improves.

Why do we need to worry about sustainability in lean systems? All of the visuals, daily huddles, focus on process, and continuous improvement we've put in place is enough, right? Wrong! Think of building your lean system as the initial months of a new healthy routine. In the very first days it is hard—you don't want to go to the gym, you don't want to wake up early, and you certainly don't want to skip dessert after dinner. But over time, you get into a routine and eventually your muscles become stronger, you lose weight, and you have more energy. This is the point where many people slip up, thinking that a day off here or there won't matter. And they don't—until the days off become greater than the days spent maintaining your new physique. Those strong muscles quickly atrophy when not exercised.

Lean systems are similar. The initial days are tough, then some gains are realized and habits start to form, and soon it feels easy. Huddles are happening, visuals are in place, managers and associates are empowered to bring up problems and use PDCA thinking to make their work better. But over time, maybe the visuals are no longer updated *every* day, perhaps schedules

CASE STUDY: MUCH ADO ABOUT NOTHING

The authors have spent a great amount of time on gemba walks at companies that have failed to build sustainability into their lean IT transformations. Inevitably the walks go something like what happened at a major regional banking company: We began in a nice conference room and heard inspirational stories guided by a slick PowerPoint presentation that painted a picture of a fantastic lean transformation. Everything from great visual management systems to collaborative environments and a problem-solving culture revealed a lean system where engaged staff were thriving and delivering value to customers. At that point we politely asked to take a walk and see it in action. Immediately we had the question, "Where's all the stuff we saw in the presentation?" The reality of their lean transformation did not match the one portrayed in the presentation. Visuals obviously hadn't been updated in weeks; the place was a library—no one was talking to each other, let alone collaborating, and the staff had actually erected makeshift barriers in their workspaces so that they didn't have to look at one another!

Digging deeper, we found that the company had implemented lean to great fanfare and had reaped many short-term benefits. But the management team had given short shrift to sustaining the lean system after *implementation*. Without this focus, the transformation became like so many other improvement programs—a flavor of the month that was quickly dying out.

So many of us managers have become great at talking about lean IT, but not so great at implementing and sustaining the system. What kind of a system are you building? The one that looks good in presentations or one that *walks the talk*?

are tight and managers no longer make time to be in the team spaces *every* day. Soon, just like the muscles of the relapsed couch potato, the lean system is not functioning. Without a system in place to ensure that the lean system sustains and improves, over time it will naturally degenerate.

Sustainability behaviors are the critical foundation in the lean house, holding up the frontline and management systems. They apply to both management and associate functions and act as the infrastructure to ensure the system is functioning as designed. This is important for a few reasons:

1. Lean systems require discipline. A constant, never-ending focus on process improvement and problem solving is tough! The sustainability system builds in a routine mechanism that ensures that what is supposed to happen actually *does* happen.
2. Your new lean system is highly visible. Stale visuals and disinterest by management send a strong signal to the organization that this is just another waning improvement program, one that any determined associate can wait out. Sustaining actions ensure that the visible elements of your system stay current.
3. Sustainability processes ensure that associates are able to get the support and coaching they need, when they need it. There may be nothing more damaging to sustainability than not providing associates the support they need to successfully reinforce new behaviors. Coaching must be frequent and planned to clear barriers and build capability.
4. Sustainability reinforces validated learning and timely course corrections as needed. Learning and discovery require practice. This can only be accomplished when the right environment is maintained while new habits are developed, shared, and eventually make their way into group and organizational culture.

The Five-Part Sustainability System

The Lean IT Sustainability System can be divided into five parts:

1. Accountability
2. Interlocking leader standard work
3. Cadenced gemba walks
4. Assessment and reflection
5. Continuous learning

Accountability

Accountability systems leverage many of the same tools and techniques we've discussed in past chapters, such as visual management, process focus, and problem solving. In this case, though, the focus is on the system itself—how it is functioning, what behaviors it is influencing, how it is improving, and how it is delivering.

Oftentimes the word *accountability* is seen in the negative light that someone must be punished for an action or problem. Holding someone accountable for a mistake at work may seem like the appropriate thing to do, but rarely does it solve the problem. In a lean transformation, accountability is not synonymous with blame. Accountability is the result of authentic respect for people—ensuring that the lean system continues to deliver value to our associates, customers, and stakeholders. Most often when expectations are not met, it is not something that people have done wrong; rather, it is the process and system that have caused the problem. Lean accountability focuses on fixing the problem—missed expectations and root causes—rather than on fixing blame for the problem. And when a problem is encountered that the team cannot solve, it is the manager's or leader's responsibility to escalate it to a level where it can be solved and to get an answer back to the team. Undesirable outcomes and missed expectations are opportunities to dig into the reasons why they occurred and develop countermeasures to improve. For someone to be held accountable, two things are requisite: a capable system and the skills, tools, and knowledge to adequately perform the work. Holding someone accountable for the performance of a broken system is the antithesis of respect for people.

In David Mann's Shingo Prize-winning book, *Creating a Lean Culture*[1] a primary feature of the daily accountability system is the tiered daily huddle, with corresponding *accountability boards* for visual management. A series of three daily meetings—one with the frontline staff, one with the manager and team leads, and one with the value stream or senior managers—are conducted and linked in order to drive understanding of the work, escalate issues, and focus on process improvements. Let's extend the idea of the daily accountability system to the foundation we built in Chapter 4.

Linking the Systems Together

The concept of the daily huddle, or standup meeting, is a familiar term to many in IT. They are a central feature of scrum or agile teams developing software. These are quick, 15 minutes-or-less meetings in which participants stand for the duration and rely on a visual management system to hold an engaged discussion. In the lean system, they also have a prominent role, and we'll expand on their use beyond the frontline and management standups you have already put into practice.

Let's take a look at an example through the incorporation of a set of linked standup meetings covering our daily activities.

- *Tier I standup*—the team standup used so often in agile software development teams. This meeting is used for what Mann calls *run-the-business* activities—those things the team needs to discuss to move the day's work forward. Topics include personal work commitments for the day, what was accomplished the prior day, and impediments to the day's work. These standups should occur at a visual management board that tracks the work flow of the team.
- *Tier II standup*—a standup meeting with the team leads or frontline managers (who have attended the Tier I meetings) and their direct managers (Tier II). This meeting focuses on escalated issues from Tier I standups, performance trends, and driving process improvements.
- *Tier III standup*—a standup meeting with the Tier II managers and the senior managers or executives (Tier III). This meeting is similar to the Tier II meeting in that it focuses on escalations, performance, and focused process improvements. The primary value of this meeting is in leaders taking swift action when teams encounter barriers to performance that are beyond the control of the managers. An equally impactful benefit is that managers and leaders are more actively involved, resolving issues on a more timely basis.

Notice the interaction between the tiers: There is always someone at the Tier II and III standups that participated in the standup at the previous level. This creates human connections that carry forward escalated problems and other concerns to higher levels of management. The highest-ranking person at each level of standup meeting, be it a team lead, manager, director, or executive, is responsible for escalating problems that cannot be solved at the level where the standup is happening. This person is also responsible for reporting the status and resolution of the problem back to the originating team. Make sure that your accountability process runs both ways—escalating issues up and reporting resolutions back down. The clarity, focus, and alignment

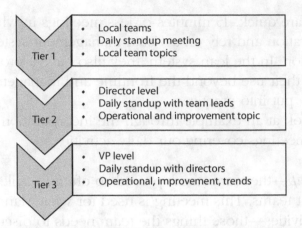

Figure 9.1 Three short meetings allow for quick, daily escalation to keep the entire organization aligned and focused on value-added work. The meetings also put in place a disciplined system to focus on continuous improvement efforts.

generated from these daily meetings are priceless! Figure 9.1 summarizes a system of tiered daily standup meetings.

The advantage of this system is that, in three short meetings, issues can be escalated from the frontline associates all the way to the executives. Each of these standups uses visual controls to track items discussed in the meeting. Ideally, the level of the discussion moves from a micro to a macro level as the discussion moves from Tier I to Tier III. Depending on the size of the organization, as you move from your model line to other areas of the organization, your situation may require more than the three tiers used in this example.

Adding Visual Accountability

Key to each of these standup meetings is visual management, with a specific focus on accountability. We've already described the importance of visual management as a cornerstone in your transformation. The lean management system has a series of reinforcing mechanisms to ensure that what is supposed to happen does happen. Visuals are an important part of this reinforcement, bringing to the surface problems, commitments, and other information of significance that might otherwise remain hidden.

Focus on getting started rather than perfecting the board before beginning. You should expect changes over time. WIP items will regularly come from the problems that are escalated and promoted by the management team. Many are items that can be solved quickly and do not require a methodical problem-solving process such as an A3. Others will require formal problem solving; in those cases be sure that an item is placed in WIP to keep the problem in focus and visual while the A3 is being worked.

In Chapter 7, we added dedicated space on the frontline and management boards for problems and the A3s used to solve them. Problems and A3s are not solely the domain of management; use care to ensure that problems are not overescalated with the new system of tiered visual management. The job of the lean manager is not to solve problems; it's to teach others how to solve problems. Ideally, problems should be solved at the level closest to where the

---

CASE STUDY: "POWER-FUL" VISUAL MANAGEMENT

At American Electric Power (AEP), one of the largest electric utilities in the United States, a multitier accountability process ensures that Chief Information Officer Alberto Ruocco and his management team stay in touch with the frontline teams' activities. This process also provides the frontline teams with a visual reminder of senior management's priorities. Each development team conducts a daily standup meeting to discuss work progress, local problem solving, items requiring escalation, and continuous improvement efforts. Ruocco leads the Tier III standup meetings, while the development manager and infrastructure manager focus on Tier II. At each tier, a visual management system is used to communicate customer-focused activities throughout IT as well as improvement leading indicators. Ruocco's visual management system is located directly outside his office, where everyone can view it easily. Says Venkat Miriyala, Director of Operations & Performance Transformation and leader of AEP IT's lean transformation, "The visual accountability system has brought a new level of understanding of key performance indicators, targets and trends, and enabled a continuous improvement mindset."

Prior to the transformation, AEP's IT organization had established metrics that were connected to the company's strategy. The recent effort focused on establishing a more comprehensive set of productivity and improvement metrics with increased visibility to frontline staff and alignment among all levels of the organization. This demonstrates a continued focus on ensuring that what is important to senior management is made visible and transparent to all. The transparency provided by visual management has helped the IT team to embed a continuous improvement mindset and to become even more effective for AEP.

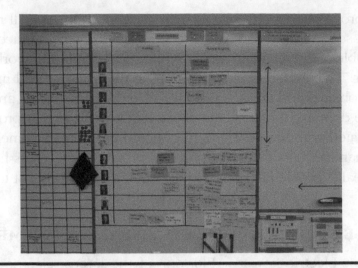

Figure 9.2   Tier IV (CTO) accountability board—Nationwide.

problem's cause is occurring. Keep this in mind as you experiment with your new system. Escalate problems when needed, but in many cases the frontline staff simply needs coaching and the authority to solve problems.

There are still other components that can be added to your board over time. Start with these suggestions and let the teams determine what other elements are needed to effectively run your accountability sessions. Don't overdo it at first—you'll be tempted to put too much on the board. Standups still need to be short 15-minute meetings; too many things on the board will take too much time to cover as well as cause the management team to lose focus. The primary purpose is to ensure that process improvement is happening, problems are being identified and resolved, and associates and managers have an effective system to escalate issues, ask for help, and get answers. You can see an example of the use of these concepts at a senior executive level in Figure 9.2. This is the board for Nationwide's Chief Technology Officer and his direct reports (including Tom!).

Interlocking Leader Standard Work

The concept of leader standard work was introduced in Chapter 5; we'll expand on the concept here by exploring the features that sustain the transformation.

Leader standard work represents the value-added work that management does on a regular basis—those things without which the operations of the organization would suffer. It ensures that people focus on the things that will make us successful for the long term, rather than constantly getting pulled into one urgent distraction after another. The phone calls, e-mails, fire drills, and other interruptions over time can prevent us from doing the work that enables our success. One of the secrets of leader standard work is that, when implemented successfully, it actually gives us more time—it is not an additional work load, but rather reserves time for leaders to focus on things that matter most, like strategy and innovation. It *creates* time for leaders by placing attention on developing our people and building problem-solving muscle in our organizations so that when the inevitable problems occur, these people are empowered and equipped to solve them.

Sustainability requires the introduction of checks and balances into leader standard work. Each successive layer of management must have activities that verify the actions and standard work of the previous level. It is critical that you not think of this verification as trying to catch someone doing something wrong. In fact, we prefer to think of this as *catching people doing things right*[2] while reinforcing focused continuous improvement. Leader standard work is directed at those activities that ensure that each layer of managers and associates is focused on what drives the engine of lean: problem solving and continuous improvement. Standards, including those for leaders, are simply a baseline on which we can (in fact, on which we must) improve on a routine basis. This is a subtlety that many people miss: Lean focuses on process, but for the purpose of improvement rather than adherence to *the way we've always done it*. The standard is just the starting point.

The methods to implement these checks are as varied as your imagination, but all should have a common element: the review of each leader's standard work with his or her manager. The specific needs of the organization as well as the level of the leader should dictate the frequency. For example, the review might be every 2 weeks for a frontline manager and his boss, but only once a month or quarterly between the CEO and CIO. The focus of this session is on the person's ability to execute standard work and to review and respond to improvement suggestions, as well as a discussion of anything that is proving to be a blocker to the shared objectives of the team. This review should be explicitly entered into every leader's standard worksheet as well.

The purpose of the review is continuous improvement. If it is used to punish staff members for not adhering to standard work, it will kill collaboration and prevent sustained change. Look for improvements and use a questioning mindset: What is preventing focus on value-added work? Who can provide coaching and help?

Cadenced Gemba Walks

We discussed earlier the importance of gemba, where the value-added work happens. It is the activities witnessed where the work is taking place that will ultimately determine whether your lean transformation is successful. It is the associates developing the software, writing the requirements, manning the support desk, and working in the trenches day in and day out that have the most direct impact on your customers. It is also the associates who amplify the culture of the company. It's puzzling why so many managers and executives avoid the gemba, feeling they have risen above the need to get into the details. Lean managers are in the details—not to micromanage—but to coach, inspire, support, and serve on a daily basis.

One challenge we often hear in IT departments is that you simply cannot walk the gemba because everything is bits and bytes and there's nothing to see. True, in many knowledge-work settings, work processes and outcomes are hidden. People often work in sequestered silos and the only way to know what is going on is to look in the system (or, rather, the only way to *think* you know what is going on is to look in the system). This is a key reason why visual management is so important in IT: to make the work flow visible and easily accessible. By now you have implemented a visual management system that serves to keep everyone up to date on current status and to create a transparent workplace of accountability. If so, you have set the foundation for constructive gemba walks that will allow you to develop a deeper understanding of the work and become a better manager and coach.

We are often reminded of the famous words of Toyota Chairman Fujio Cho,[3] "Go see, ask why, show respect," as a great model of how gemba walks should work. Many of the concepts applied to your transformation come through in Chairman Cho's words:

1. *Coaching*—the act of asking why and moving toward incremental improvement is critical to coaching. Effective coaching is less about telling than it is about listening and asking effective questions. Coach for improvement, not correction.
2. *Respect for people*—simply going to the gemba and asking a bunch of questions is not respecting people. The questions must be phrased in such a way to respect the contributions of associates, build trust, and drive continuous improvement. Great coaching focuses on the process: what should be happening versus what is happening, rather than on who is to blame.

3. *Disciplined management*—associates see and emulate the actions of management; if the lean system is not important enough for the management team to review and examine on a regular basis, it will soon lose importance for the associates team as well.

Gemba walks are focused activities with a specific purpose: to scrutinize and deeply understand work progress and process improvement activities. They are not *management by walking around* or a chance to gather all the associates to listen to the management team—what we call *shaking hands and kissing babies* syndrome. The gemba walk is all about the associates and their work and not about the executives or the management team. Perhaps the most difficult thing for leaders to do when taking a gemba walk is to leave their egos behind. As a general rule, if leaders and managers are doing more than 30%–40% of the talking, the gemba walk is not effective at engaging people to create a culture of daily team-based problem solving.

The specifics may have to be adjusted based on your organization's structure, but in general, structure your gemba walks in the following way:

■ *Level 1: Daily*—local-level manager with his team leads or a subset of the team. The purpose is to review the visuals, coach, and allow issue escalation. Care must be taken to ensure this is an empowering activity for the team and not micromanaging.
■ *Level 2: Daily or weekly*—senior manager or director with each of his or her managers. The purpose is to study the performance visuals, coach, and follow up on improvement projects.
■ *Level 3: Weekly or monthly*—executive with each of his or her directors/ senior managers. The purpose is to scrutinize the visuals, coach, and follow up on improvement projects.

You can see a repeating pattern at each level, with focus on visuals and coaching. The gemba walks serve to reinforce the clarity and communication of the daily standup meetings. The difference lies in their focus: The daily standup is a general report in, lasts about 15 minutes, and primarily focuses on daily issues of work and improvement. The gemba walk centers on assessing the depth of engagement of the teams, the degree to which lean systems are being actively used, and opportunities for leaders and managers to support and coach.

The point of the gemba walk is to see things as they really are—not in a report, not in a status meeting, not in a conversation with the project manager, but from where the value-added work is occurring. The essence of a great gemba walk is to see things from the perspective of the associates! This can be at an agile team space, functional work area, data center—anywhere within the IT organization where work is being done that is creating value for customers. Within our world of technology, the product or service being created cannot always be easily observed. This is why the use of visual management is so important. It is a representation of the work that is happening, a proxy of sorts that stands in for the product. Without it, oftentimes both management and associates fail to get value from the walks and they degenerate or stop altogether.

Gemba walks should be scheduled and posted on the manager's cadence calendar (e.g., leader standard work). These walks must be held as sacrosanct; they need to occur as planned and on time. This is one of the most visible lean management practices and reinforces the importance of the lean system to frontline management and associates, acting as a reinforcing mechanism. The manager responsible for the area being walked should lead the walk and take notes on improvement actions.

To ensure that the management team stays on task with the walks, we recommend the use of a gemba walk checklist. Provide a checklist, or standard work for gemba walks, to guide the management team as they participate on their walks. A simple checklist will go a long way to ensuring that managers go to the gemba with a purpose and make it an empowering process for everyone involved.

Assessment and Reflection

Some tough news for all of us: Over 70% of these types of transformations fail.[4] A great many of these failures could be avoided if lean leaders took a step back and applied the same principles they deployed in their organizations to the transformation process itself: namely, problem solving and continuous improvement. One way to do that is to regularly assess, reflect, and apply countermeasures to the transformation.

Personal Reflection

A critical element of any lean leader is *hansei*, or self-reflection. Taking the time for introspection to understand the impact that we, as lean leaders, have on the people, processes, and the systems around us is critical to improving our personal leadership capability and our capacity for coaching others. The same applies to the lean transformation as a whole. We should always be on watch in our daily jobs, with kaizen eyes, watching out for waste and opportunities to improve, learn, and teach. But we often fail to step back and look at the big picture of the transformation—asking what the ultimate purpose is. Are we moving toward our True North? What changes are required to continue improving? Each transformation is situational in context, and the tools and principles that apply and work best are different in each one. Further, as you progress and mature, the focus of the transformation will shift. A lean transformation is never complete; it merely adapts to the current challenges and opportunities of the organization. While this field guide gives you a roadmap to start your transformation, ultimately your adaptation of these principles to the obstacles you encounter will be the determining factor of whether or not you are successful.

Reflection is necessary to making informed and effective adaptations. For a lean leader, a good start is to reflect on the five "Ps": Purpose, Process, People, Problem Solving, and Personal Leadership. Focusing on these areas and aligning them to the True North goals you have identified for your organization and transformation will keep you on the right path. This does not have to be a complicated process and should be a part of your standard work, occurring on a regular basis. The key point is to set a regular cadence for self-examination with yourself and your team.

Lean System Assessment

One input to the reflection process is formal and informal assessments of the lean system. From accountability meetings to interlocking leader standard work, you are probably discerning that a lot of counterbalances are needed in your new system to prevent atrophy. It's a little bit of a paradox: On the one hand, we are empowering our associates and giving them more control over their daily work and improvement of their work; on the other, we continually check and monitor the system to see if what we are expecting to happen actually is happening. This is really quite logical when taking into account the cultural changes occurring along with the process changes—namely, that our work is a daily experiment that we're striving to constantly improve. Effective experiments require data. The assessment process is simply data to measure how the system is functioning and an opportunity to keep the focus on continuous improvement of both the work and the way work is done.

In a way, assessments are happening every day. Review of standard work, gemba walks, and the daily accountability standups are all designed to review lean and work processes to provide a chance for coaching and developing our people. An important part of the job of a lean manager is to learn and to teach others what the manager has discovered along the way.

We have found, however, that these daily activities are simply not enough in most companies to sustain the journey. Deeper looks into the system, with the results stored to identify and understand trends, are needed to continue the journey. Similarly to the reflection process described in "Assessment and Reflection," these deep dives should occur on a regular basis and become a part of standard work for the organization. They should be based on carefully chosen metrics to ensure that we are making decisions based on accurate information.

Metrics and measures are absolutely important in determining the effectiveness of the delivery of products and services to our customers, whether it's software, support services, networks, servers, defect fixes, or anything else. None of us would consider running our organizations without them. Things such as our productivity levels, defects, and service-level agreement fulfillment serve as measuring sticks and indicators of performance. We can also collect measurements on the transformation and use them as guideposts for improvement or corrective action. For example, in measuring the lean transformation, we're assessing the practices and principles that guide us to see if they are taking root within the organization—becoming a part of our DNA and ensuring continuous improvement.

For the transformation metrics, we must focus on leading (predictive) indicators instead of the lagging indicators so often used in our organizations. Defects, productivity, project success, availability, and other standard IT metrics look in the rearview mirror. They are important, but at the same time it is hard to drive forward when you are only looking backward at historical performance. For the transformation metrics you must look at the critical elements you have put in place with the expectation that these new processes and principles will lead to better results, even if it does not happen right away. Table 9.1 shows a few examples of leading indicators you can measure as part of an ongoing assessment routine.

Continuous Learning

The prior components of the sustainability system—accountability, interlocking leader standard work, cadenced gemba walks, assessment, and

Table 9.1 Potential Metrics for Ongoing Assessments of the Lean Journey

Category	Measure	Intent
People	Skills: track the attainment of needed skills by person/group visually with target dates	Ensure that you are providing associates and managers the tools, training, and support they need to be successful in their jobs
People	Coaching: time spent coaching and effectiveness of the coaching sessions	The primary role of leaders in the lean system is to coach and instill learning and self-discovery
Process	Standups: attendance and effectiveness	Standups are a primary communication and escalation method of the lean system
Process	Cadence calendar: how often does the cadence calendar accurately reflect what is happening in the workplace?	Cadence calendars create repeatable management behaviors designed to build predictability in the organization
Process	Standard work: is standard work followed? Is standard work constantly being improved?	Baselines are known and improving; innovation and continuous improvement
Problem solving	A3s: are they used? Are they improving work processes, the lean system, and standard work? Are problems being identified and worked?	Continuous improvement; problem-solving culture
Personal leadership	Are leaders actively practicing hansei and sharing their learning, setbacks, and successes with peers?	Personal growth and collaboration among leadership

reflection—are all designed to allow the leaders of the lean transformation to continually learn and improve the system through their own actions and through the empowering of associates and managers. This happens through observation, coaching, and experimentation. This concept of continuous learning must permeate all aspects of the new lean system. Above all else, a lean thinker is a learner. When we put aside our egos as leaders, acknowledge that we do not know everything, and accept that most of the time our associates know more than we do about our processes, we can truly become learners.

In fact, learning should be a part of every aspect of your lean transformation, including lean processes, daily work, strategy, and execution. You must create a mindset centered on continuous learning within all team members.[5] The power of moving from an organization where everyone just does his or her job to one where people do their jobs *and* find ways to improve their jobs cannot be overstated. Information technology changes so rapidly that you cannot possibly anticipate what the landscape will look like in 2–3 years, let alone 5–10 years. But what you can anticipate and improve is the ability of your organization to adapt to the coming changes, whatever they may be. Create the learning ecosystem now that will ensure that everyone is able to continue to provide value well into the future. A case study follows of how Nationwide created a practitioner-led learning system without heavy investment.

Creating the opportunities for frontline associates, managers, and leaders to learn and grow is of paramount importance. This will not happen without intentionally focused effort. Your job as a lean leader is to use the tools available to you in order to create opportunities for continuous learning. All of the components of the sustainability system will put you on the right path. Remember the maxim that every day is an experiment; creating a culture of continuous learning is the embodiment of this principle.

Sustainability Wrap-Up

Lean transformations are not a project; they create a new way of working. Without a committed focus to changing foundational elements of the organization—baking the changes into the DNA of the company—lean will not have a lasting impact. Building sustainability into the transformation from the beginning will provide a tremendous advantage as you progress. And while taking the time now may seem difficult, it's much easier than the rework necessary when the system falls apart from lack of support structures. Make the commitment to build a legacy of lean leadership and execution in your transformation by implementing the five-part sustainability system described in this chapter.

CASE STUDY: TEACHING THURSDAYS[6]

Nationwide's IT department, an 8000+ person organization, encountered a common problem within enterprise IT: keeping the skills of associates relevant in a changing technology landscape. The organization was undergoing rapid change, moving from legacy technologies and custom development to an environment of new technology and package applications. Traditional training programs did not seem to be keeping pace and associates were largely unsatisfied with the offerings available to them.

Introduced earlier, Nationwide IT had already embarked on a lean and agile transformation within the application development organization. Collaborative teams and workspaces, continuous improvement, and a culture of empowered and engaged associates had already been largely embraced. Still, the skills the development workforce possessed were rapidly eroding and would not be sufficient to carry the company forward. The company had no intention of simply terminating existing associates and hiring new staff with the skills needed. This was an opportunity for senior management to show their commitment to associates and demonstrate respect for people.

Understanding that management is often behind the curve in knowing what training the developers, testers, analysts, and project managers need, Nationwide created an associate-driven program for its application development groups that had just one rule:

> Every other Thursday from 1:30 p.m. to 3:30 p.m. everyone is either teaching, learning in a teaching session, or developing material to teach.

It's that simple—practitioner led, management supported, and simple to understand. The management team put in place the support to schedule the rooms, published the schedule, and let associates take care of the rest. In 2014, the development organization had over 150 teaching sessions and over 8000 participants—that's a lot of learning! Further, the associates were teaching the skills the company needed, without management intervention—a great example of what happens when you empower people to obtain the skills they need to be successful in their jobs.

Notes

1. David Mann, *Creating a Lean Culture: Tools to Sustain Lean Conversions* (Boca Raton, FL: CRC Press, 2005).
2. Adapted in this context from R. Gary Butler, Executive-in-Residence, Fisher College of Business, The Ohio State University, and his teaching of "moving from trying to find things that are wrong to looking for compelling evidence that things are right."
3. Many works exist that reference Mr. Cho's famous words; the authors recommend one of John Shook's eLetters "How to Go to the Gemba: Go See, Ask Why, Show Respect" on lean.org as a good starting point.
4. Scott Keller and Colin Price, *Beyond Performance: How Great Organizations Build Ultimate Competitive Advantage* (Hoboken, NJ: John Wiley & Sons, 2011).
5. One of the best works on the rewards of having a learning-oriented mindset is Carol Dweck's book: *Mindset: The New Psychology of Success* (Ballantine Books, 2006).
6. Thanks to Tim Lyons, Chief Information Security Officer, Nationwide, and Kathleen Bryan, Director, IT Process Management, Nationwide, for their contribution to this case study.

Chapter 10

The Importance
of Strategic Alignment

Empowerment without alignment is chaos.

Peter Senge[1]
The Fifth Discipline, 1990

Introduction

At this point in your journey, you have come a long distance, working hard
to implement a lean IT system for both frontline associates and management. You have created the building blocks necessary for a strong foundation. This chapter extends the transformation model to the creation and
execution of your organization's strategic imperatives.

Purpose-Driven Alignment

In Chapter 3, "The Importance of Purpose," we highlighted the clarity of
your True North as a precondition for your people to engage and perform
at their best. It is *necessary* for everyone in the company to understand the
ultimate reasons why the company exists and how their work directly contributes to its objectives. When everyone is moving toward a common cause
and when all members of a team, department, and company are aligned, it

is much easier to execute and achieve the mission. That's because much of the wasteful activity associated with a lack of coordination and collaboration is eliminated. Imagine playing on a soccer team where each player was not collaborating with the other players or aligned to the ultimate purpose of the game. Chaos would ensue. Why do we expect anything different from our own teams? *Alignment* is the most common oversight we encounter in companies struggling to create a work environment and culture that engages people and fosters lean behavior.

Creation of a great mission statement or articulating True North is not enough. You must go a step further and ensure that everyone—from the janitor to the executives—understands and uses True North to drive the execution of strategy in his or her daily work. In our visits to other companies, it is common to find fewer than 10% of the people with a clear understanding of their organization's strategy, let alone how their work affects it. It is estimated that 85% of executive teams spend less than 1 hour per month discussing strategy.

Often strategy is something defined by leadership, shared annually with directors and managers, and then trickled down to associates on a need-to-know basis. Plans are developed at a strategic level while projects are identified at the tactical level, but no clear connection between the two is explicitly made. This leaves people to individually interpret company strategy and how their work furthers those ends, all but guaranteeing a lack of agreement and common understanding. Left to their own devices, people either do their best to infer what they should be working on to support company strategy or they may not even consider how their work relates to the company's ultimate intentions.

Think of your company as an orchestra. You can have the world's best musicians, but without a conductor (e.g., leadership) focusing on a common piece of music (e.g., strategy) it is very unlikely that everyone is making music by contributing toward a common purpose and shared objectives. Strategy provides clarity and agreement on what is most important, aligned to True North.

Perhaps the most impactful aspect of a well-deployed strategy is what it helps people *not* to do! It's this deadly combination of working on the wrong things (firefighting and immediate crises) plus multitasking that cripples our ability to deliver on strategic goals. The strategic plan becomes the prioritization mechanism used to determine if the new *fire* should be put out or addressed at all. A clear purpose-based strategy empowers people to identify those things they should stop doing in order to focus on activities that more fully support common objectives.

What Is Strategy Deployment?

The ability to effectively create, communicate, deploy, and align strategy plays a critical role in your evolution toward enterprise excellence. The challenge of aligning people around a common objective has thwarted many companies from realizing their strategic goals, so it comes as no surprise that the lean body of knowledge has tools and methods to address this need, referred to as *strategy deployment*. First, we need to make a distinction between strategy and deployment.

A strategy is a plan of action designed to achieve a major or overall objective or goal. Strategies typically have a multiyear plan or vision of where an organization needs to be by a specific time in the future. The goal of developing a strategy is to create clarity of how to realize the purpose of an organization.

Strategy deployment is typically a 1-year plan as well as a process used to distill your organization's purpose into short-term actionable goals from which we can assign importance, responsibility, and resources, and then measure progress. In many ways, strategy deployment is the central nervous system of the lean management system you've been building as you have worked through this book. It provides four critical elements:

1. It drives activity across silos and addresses organizational value-stream-level improvements required to support the strategic plan. The focus is on significantly *moving the needle* on a few big things rather than slight improvements of many small things.
2. It reinforces people at all levels of the organization to actively apply PDCA thinking as the basis of all improvement work.[2] It includes all levels of management in figuring out the *how*, once the organizational *what* has been determined.
3. It emphasizes a monthly review mechanism for all to see, know, and act, focusing exclusively on those things not on track and specific countermeasures to get back on course.
4. It creates a closed-loop feedback between organizational purpose/ strategy and daily activities at an individual, team, department, and enterprise level. Strategic planning starts *before*—not after—the financial budget process.[3]

You may have heard the Japanese term *hoshin kanri* used in place of strategy deployment. *Hoshin* means management. *Kanri* is translated as direction,

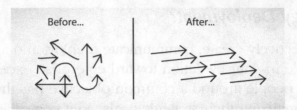

Figure 10.1   Chaos versus alignment.

shining needle, or vision compass, which helps keep the organization moving toward its True North. We feel the term that best describes what we are trying to accomplish is *strategy alignment*. In the end, all strategic planning, management, and deployment will deliver results when we successfully align purpose with the understanding and actions of everyone in the organization.

When those closest to the work define and cultivate iterative improvement cycles toward common goals, alignment of strategy and daily work begins to take hold up, down, and across the enterprise. Figure 10.1 provides a simple but effective depiction of the power of strategic alignment.

A Path to Implementation

Implementing strategy alignment is not for the timid. It requires commitment to the lean system by all levels in the organization and a willingness to have open, frank, and often difficult conversations. It places an increased burden on executives to understand and define where the organization needs to go and challenges the entire workforce to come together and make progress toward those goals every day.

Step 1—Develop the Plan/Create the Challenge

The purpose and vision of your company is to inform and clarify strategy. The strategy defines *what* we need to accomplish this year to move closer to fulfilling our purpose. Leveraging the power of lean thinking and PDCA, think of strategy as a scientific hypothesis. If we successfully implement the strategy, what impact will it have on our customers, employees, suppliers, and community? Strategy tends to define the *what*, but not the *how*. To be effective, a clear link between high-level strategies and tactical projects must be made. PDCA is extremely effective at assisting people to establish this link. The strategy alignment process enlists everyone in your organization to take part in the experiment. The key is to get people excited about doing so!

Try to envision the impact of effectively linking your strategy to the True North idea of operational excellence. It is through ongoing continuous improvement efforts (kaizen) that people make the many small-step improvements required to support their strategic objectives. We say *their objectives* because, when everyone sees the strategy as something that he or she owns, everyone actively participates in its construction. At this point, we may understand the *what*, but we have barely begun to grasp the *how* of realizing our strategy.

Your company strategy may include the introduction of new products and services, expansion into new markets, and/or the adoption of new technologies. Whatever the organizational strategy is, the task of IT leadership is to answer the questions (1) "What strategy should IT deploy to support and enable the company strategy?" and (2) "What information and functionality need to be operational to put people in a position to successfully mobilize our company strategy?" These questions require a deep understanding that is only developed when IT *goes and sees* to grasp how the business is using information and technology, *appreciates* the challenges people are facing, *comprehends* what end users are trying to optimize, and deeply *understands* how users use IT to do their work.

This happens when IT actively participates in the strategic planning process with *every other* functional group (HR, finance, legal, compliance, operations, marketing, sales, supply chain, etc.). There will be many separate business projects, IT projects, and process improvement projects, but they will be aligned to become components of one strategic plan to achieve a shared future vision. The key is that your people see themselves and their work as part of a single integrated plan.

Step 2—Deploy the Plan: Nested Cycles of PDCA

The core practice that drives alignment, accountability, and follow-through is a deceptively challenging practice called *catchball*. Executives define the strategic direction and high-level measurable targets to be achieved, and then share them with their direct reports. Each successive level in the organization is then asked to answer the questions, "What is your plan to make this happen?" "Can you explain how it will be accomplished, when it will happen, and by whom?" "What resources do you require to be successful?"

In other words, leaders in the organization set goals and each supporting level comes up with quantifiable objectives and plans to achieve them. At

WHAT ABOUT THE X-MATRIX?

If you have done some reading on strategy deployment, you have no doubt come across a tool called the X-matrix. When used properly, this tool enables leaders to effectively construct and align strategic goals, tactics, accountability, and measurements. When used improperly, the X-matrix becomes a tedious, mind-numbing distraction costing many hours of effort and resulting in little alignment or measurable results.

For IT organizations (or companies) that are just beginning a lean journey, we find that initially focusing on the X-matrix tool is *not* effective in building strategy or sustaining alignment. The discipline and maturity required by the tool simply do not yet exist in these organizations. The power of strategy alignment is lost as people focus on the format and rules of the process. In our experience, you don't need to introduce the X-matrix to achieve strategic alignment. Once you have been actively pursuing alignment as a part of your lean IT transformation, by all means take a look at the X-matrix[4] to see if it is a tool your organization can use to drive higher levels of alignment and coordination. We suggest you approach this as you would any other experiment and ask: "Within the context of strategic alignment, how will this tool help to close the gap between what should be happening and what is currently happening?"

that point the dialogue begins! The strategy and goals are delivered *top-down* while the plans to get there are generated *bottom-up*. When done effectively, this messy[5] process creates plans and measurable targets that are owned by the people who create them and aligned with the organization's purpose, objectives, and strategy!

The art of catchball is spending enough time to ensure alignment of strategy and daily work while not wasting time on details that are sure to change once work is begun, problems encountered, and learning takes place. If conversations are respectful and crisp, people will see value in them and actively engage—furthering identification with purpose and greater alignment!

Ideas (goals and quantifiable objectives) generated at one level of an organization are shared with people at the next supporting level. Those people and teams receiving the ideas are expected to adjust them to make them relevant to the work done at their level and to pass them along to the next level. Figure 10.2 shows how each cycle of catchball is nothing less significant than a PDCA cycle. Think of each level of the organization engaging

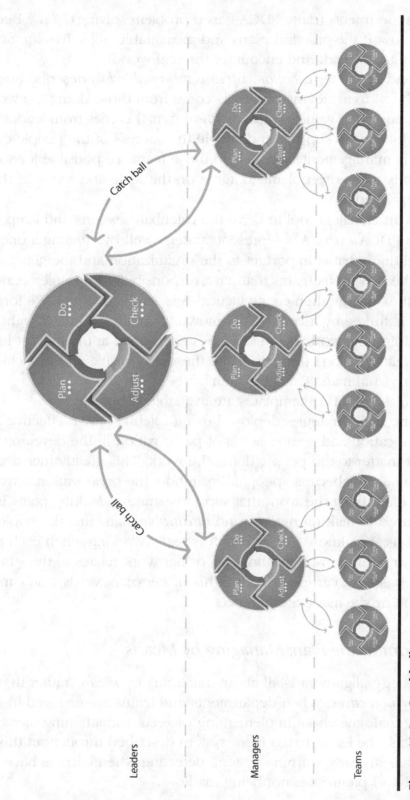

Figure 10.2 Catchball process.

in ongoing experiments (daily PDCA-based problem solving). Why? Because we do not know if the practical plans and measurable objectives are achievable until we get to work and encounter the real world!

Mike is fond of the term *bottom-up and top-enabled* to describe how the *means* (how) to achieving our goals come from those doing the work and creating customer value, while *direction* (what) comes from leadership, whose job it is to support and enable the success of the people doing the work. It is management's job to help those teams responsible for solving strategically aligned problems to agree on the scale and scope of the improvements needed.

The A3 is an excellent tool to drive the catchball sessions and keep the focus on the PDCA cycle. A3s represent strategy well by creating a one-page view highlighting what is important to the organization and the general plan to get there. Various teams that have responsibility for implementing portions of the strategy then create tactical A3s. The individual A3s form a scheme that is linked by a common framework, creating a line of sight from the people doing the work to the strategies envisioned at the highest levels in the organization. Don't forget to make these A3s visible and to include them in your visual management system.

Strategy and tactical A3 templates are available at our site.

When done well, strategies deployed using catchball drive effective two-way communication and greater levels of participation in the development of goals that matter to the people doing the work. This greatly increases the likelihood of success because people throughout the organization actively take part in identifying the work that supports strategy. Making plans is easy when compared to making *realistic* and *attainable* plans that fit people's work situations. You know that catchball is really working when each person in your organization knows how his or her work relates to the strategic goals of the business, can describe it in his or her own words, and can show you where he or she made a difference!

Step 3—Monitor the Plan: Managing by Means

Effective strategy alignment is all about managing by *means* rather than managing by *objectives*. When departments and teams are engaged in ongoing two-way dialogue about implementing projects and attaining measurable objectives, the lean management system described throughout this book serves as an early warning system, detecting when barriers have been encountered and progress is not being made.

Many leaders lack the capability to translate desired outcomes into actionable plans for improvement. In fact, the leader's job is to describe the desired outcomes of the strategy in such a way that managers and supporting teams begin to see a path from where they are now to where they need to be.

Look for clear linkages between strategic measures and the measures of related supporting improvement efforts. This is an effective way to assess whether teams are aligned in their purpose and focusing on the right improvement work. It is also useful to ask, "What behaviors do these measurements drive and are they behaviors which further our strategic objectives?"

We become what we think about and focus on most often. Vigorous monitoring of activity and tracking progress are essential to maintaining momentum. If you stop tracking your progress, the energy of alignment will wither and die very quickly because the *tyranny of the urgent* will absorb the attention and energy of your people and reactive crises management will again be the order of the day. Monitoring progress keeps what is most important (realizing the strategy) at the forefront, so it is at the center in people's daily focus.

Take the time now to build monitoring of strategy execution into leader standard work. Put the strategy and tactics on your visual management system and schedule regular monthly reviews that coincide with your assessment of financial and lean key performance indicators (KPIs). Be prepared to coach people through inevitable problems, changes, and opportunities. Carefully monitoring and adapting your strategic alignment and improvement process is one of the most powerful features of your lean system.

Step 4—Improve the System: Nested Subcycles of PDCA

It is helpful to think of strategy deployment and alignment as a series of cascading initiatives, from the business as a whole, to value streams, to specific business units, to sites, to departments, and finally to teams.[6] If your teams are not engaging daily in PDCA discussions around projects and improvements directly tied to strategic goals, you can be assured there is no substantive progress being made or alignment of effort toward your strategic goals!

Use leader standard work to reinforce the importance of reviewing progress and post the findings using the visual management system. This provides an opportunity to check and adjust problem-solving activities aimed to achieve elements of the strategy. Strategic alignment is not about getting it right the first time out; that's not realistic. It is about creating a vertically aligned system of continuous improvement. Adding a standard work component to review strategic progress on a regular cadence is necessary; otherwise, the focus will quickly fade. Go and see management, making things visual, meaningful measures, standard work, and structured problem solving combine to detect, check, and adjust the means as necessary.

Daily tasks that are explicitly connected with strategy are the vital work that must be done at the highest level of performance. The degree of experimentation and adjustment in connection with this daily work indicates the commitment to excellence that people are making. This thoughtful dedication can be seen through the consistent practice of PDCA structured problem solving.

Take another look at Figure 10.2. The PDCA cycles occurring at the team level need to occur daily in order for your organization to experience the necessary learning required to realize measurable gains in support of strategic goals. A review of any team's visual boards and A3s reveals a story about the degree to which strategy is influencing daily work and to which focus is shifting from reactive firefighting to more impactful issues with long-term consequences.

This Isn't Easy!

As you consider these basic stages of developing, deploying, monitoring, and improving the rollout of your strategic initiatives, you may be thinking, "This is straightforward and simply a matter of execution!" Well, yes and no—it is simple to describe and understand, but it is wickedly difficult to build widespread *everybody, everyday* engagement. In fact, most strategy deployment efforts we have seen fall far short of achieving the organizational alignment and measurable progress needed to achieve the goals of the organization. The question is, "Why?" The following are some things to watch out for as you enter this phase of your transformation:

- *Lack of understanding and practice*—neither fully appreciating the importance of alignment (the why) nor understanding the mechanics and the level of commitment required (the what).
- *Not letting go of command and control*—failing to acquire and practice lean leadership skills such as facilitative leadership, team-based dialogue, and new paradigms of what it means to lead people.

- *No differentiation between planning and deployment*—most companies are skilled at planning and weak at executing. If you don't see these two practices as necessitating different mindsets, skill sets, and tool sets, you are going to encounter problems.
- *Wind the clock (set it and forget it) mentality*—thinking that the strategy alignment process will sustain itself without ongoing monitoring and adjustments as setbacks are encountered. The emergent complexity inherent in business makes active vigilance of the deployment process an absolute necessity.
- *Leave it to the experts*—abdicating responsibility to an internal continuous improvement team or outside consultants for managing and sustaining strategy alignment efforts is a recipe for failure. Experts may be able to help but leaders must lead.
- *No work systems to reinforce behavior*—failing to leverage standard work, visual management, go and see, and measures to accurately monitor, assess, and fine-tune the progressive realization of strategy to focus and enable daily work.
- *Lost in translation*—using terminology and processes that are overly complicated and alienate people so that they do not experience the value of strategy alignment.

So What Does It Look Like in Practice?

An example may be helpful here. Let's say you are the CIO of a large company. The company's executive leadership creates the annual strategic plan for the business, which includes several key measurable targets. As the CIO it is your job to translate what the business strategy means to IT and how your organization can further the mission of the company.

The company's strategy includes the following targets:

- Growth in existing markets: +10%
- Growth from new market expansion: +5%
- Improved levels of customer satisfaction: +20%
- Revenue targets: +10%
- Employee retention: +20%
- Operating costs: −7%

Let's take a look at how you might align the customer satisfaction target within IT.

Develop the Plan

As CIO, you gather your leadership team and task them with translating strategic targets into actionable tactics that IT staff can work toward. You ask your direct reports to attend and actively participate in the catchball sessions of the business leaders and stakeholders they support to understand what the business is trying to achieve in *its* plans. The direct reports use their observations to play catchball with you (the CIO) to formulate an IT strategy that aligns with and complements what the business is trying to realize. For example, having reflected on your company's intent to significantly improve customer satisfaction, you distill the 20% improvement target to a corresponding IT strategy: strengthen partnerships between the business and IT.

Your leader standard work calls for you to create an A3 supporting strengthening the IT partnership with the business. It includes how you will measure progress and the high-level plans that will be employed to achieve success. You develop this with your leadership team, who will correspondingly share the A3 with their managers in supporting catchball sessions with successive levels of IT. The directors ask managers to work with their teams to identify (and capture on an A3) the specific activities and measurable targets each department intends to pursue in support of this strategic goal. Their specific tactical A3s become aligned with what was learned by the directors while sitting in on the business's catchball sessions!

With this approach, IT strategy becomes an element of the business's strategic plan and not just a stand-alone, siloed IT plan. As an added bonus, it also replaces the traditional IT intake process of gathering project portfolio ideas for next year.

Deploy the Plan

The next step in your process is to deploy the plan throughout your organization. All departments that will be involved in the work to achieve this target should provide feedback on the A3 and, if needed, develop a supporting A3 to plan their experiments to move the company toward realizing the goal.

Each area develops a specific experiment (based on PDCA problem solving) to further the progress. An A3 is created to capture the problem/opportunity that each area is trying to address, the current state, and baseline measures. Teams within the department create their own A3s, which will reinforce and underpin the department's A3 (some refer to these as a parent and child A3s). It is important to note that, at this point, each tactical A3 represents an experiment the team is undertaking to achieve specific performance targets. There will certainly be setbacks and problems along the way and PDCA thinking will facilitate thoughtful course corrections and countermeasures. Figure 10.2 represents this process of cascading A3s, all moving the company closer to the stated goal through a series of interconnected experiments.

For example, one of your development teams, Web Services, which is a part of Application Services, creates an A3 with the problem statement, "Customer needs are not fully understood prior to application launches." Assume that the Web Services A3 is aligned to the Application Services A3, which is aligned to the CIO's A3. The Web Services team manager uses catchball to challenge the team to understand the current situation, identify measures, and analyze potential root causes in order to develop promising countermeasures—all with the intent of creating alignment between what the team is trying to accomplish and the associated strategic goal. A great question to ask here is, "How will the team's success in addressing this problem further our strategic goals?"

This process is repeated as all departments and supporting teams create a network of cascading A3s that illustrate the connectedness of the improvement work in flight. When made visible, it is relatively easy to see any gaps in the alignment of projects and action designated as most important.

Monitor the Plan

As the teams begin to frame their improvement efforts in support of strategic goals, A3s become a central element of the visual management system and progress is actively measured and monitored. *This is where many companies experience a breakdown in the strategic deployment process.* If you do not bake your strategy into your daily lean management system (standard work, visual management, go and see, leader standard work, measurements, and PDCA), it will not become the central focus of your people. They may be actively engaged in improvement work, but it is unlikely to be work intentionally aligned with the strategic objectives of your organization!

Improve the System

As teams make headway on their improvement efforts, the focus expands to include verification that progress is being made and gains made support the measurable goals of the parent strategy. It is during this *confirmation of alignment* that we make course corrections to the lean management and strategy deployment systems to orient all improvement efforts toward

CASE STUDY: A TALE OF ALIGNMENT

CI&T is a global software company, with lean embedded at its core. The name CI&T is from the founding principles of collaboration, innovation, and transformation. Leading complex digital transformations for global enterprises, CI&T's skilled teams have been called unflappable problem solvers and experts at mastering new technologies using lean and agile methodologies—all while navigating the unique challenges of the enterprise customer.

CI&T started its lean journey in 2007 with the intent to enhance its agile practices. Lean quickly seeped into the company culture, providing a foundation for a shared mindset of business value, as well as a process to learn, improve, and tackle the unpredictable challenges faced in its business environment. After experimentation, the company had a series of successes and lean quickly permeated CI&T with an obsession for continuous improvement. In 2010, senior leadership embraced hoshin kanri (strategy deployment) and this provided organizational alignment in driving enterprise transformation.

As the *CI&T Production System* became established, monthly strategy review sessions were implemented using A3 as a communication tool to ensure alignment throughout the organization. A3s are used at all levels of the organization and deliver an accessible way to talk about and understand strategic execution. Senior leaders begin the annual process of discussing and creating the hoshin (plan), including enterprise-level hypotheses and countermeasures. They then share this information throughout the organization, using kickoff meetings, presented by senior leadership, in each division. In addition, each division hosts a monthly "What's Going On" session focusing on strategy, progress to plan, and cultural metrics. Functional leads also have monthly PDCA cycles to report progress and how their groups are performing. To keep things front and center, the CEO reports quarterly on key indicators, including financials, tying them back to strategy deployment and alignment.

While strategy is set at the executive level, leadership actively encourages autonomy and problem solving by the teams at the execution level. This is accomplished using catchball sessions to determine how the teams intend to actualize the strategy. Part of the company's success seems to emanate from a nonadversarial environment. The system is very inclusive; leadership is committed to a role of enabling efficient work flow and has a saying to encourage openness and problem solving: "Face the brutal facts!"

CI&T's experience deploying and aligning strategy has been a game changer in accelerating the company's transformation to Operational Excellence. With a company-wide understanding that the value and impact of lean is driven by the teams themselves, CI&T CEO César Gon instituted the company mantra: "We develop people before we develop software."

common goals. Improvements to the system are always performed using A3s and PDCA problem solving.

Why Not Talk about Strategy Sooner?

Policy deployment and alignment is a process by which the vision and goals of the organization are shared in a way that positions everyone to act in coordinated support of those goals. Leveraging the power of lean and PDCA, think of strategy as a scientific hypothesis—a series of aligned, nested if–then experiments. While it is one of the most powerful components of the lean system, it is also very difficult to implement, especially when your journey has just begun.

It is senseless to introduce strategy deployment before your people are prepared. Until you have positioned a lean management system and developed the behavioral habits to create change toward common goals, there is little capability to align people toward a common purpose. Allow them time to gain a comfort level with the visual management system, daily huddles, A3 problem solving, and standard work before you emphasize strategy alignment.

What about Major Strategic Breakthroughs?

Before you task people to achieve major breakthroughs, it is wise to master the basic blocking and tackling skills of lean and embed the behaviors of daily problem solving. To this end, spend the first year or two developing your strategy deployment system with a focus on small- to medium-size problems that impact the business. There is never a shortage of these chronic issues that could be solved if we only invested the time to address them. People should learn new routines of behavior and thinking—and the results they generate—before attempting to take on major innovation and breakthrough discovery. Until you have laid the groundwork, going after a strategic breakthrough may prove to be a fool's errand.

Once teams demonstrate a foundation of problem solving, senior leadership may identify a few large breakthrough challenges (no more than three) for the organization. Be careful to pull back if you discover that teams lack the communication and coordination skills required to manage these enterprise value-stream-level initiatives. We've encountered this problem several times. People develop the skills necessary to tackle departmental problems, but find they are quickly out of their depth when taking on system-level challenges often associated with breakthrough and radical change. Again, leadership plays a critical role in demonstrating the collaboration and coordination essential to impact value-stream performance. While the potential return from such initiatives may be promising, the visibility and risk of these undertakings can be massive. Proceed with caution!

Central Nervous System—The Power of Alignment

The ability to create, communicate, deploy, and align strategy plays a critical role in your evolution toward enterprise excellence. Strategy alignment is all about engaging managers and frontline workers to actively partake in ongoing tactical execution and problem solving around common themes that *matter most*. When done well, strategy deployment has the ability to accelerate change and fuel transformation. As decisive and aligned learning occurs, the power of continuously improving people and processes grows almost exponentially. Orienting everyone in your organization toward a shared purpose while providing the means with which to achieve measurable progress will propel you ahead of the competition and produce a potent competitive advantage.

Although there are a variety of models and methods associated with achieving strategic alignment, the real challenge lies in your organization's collective ability for team members to respectfully connect and communicate with one another to experiment and learn, align purpose with action, and pivot when a course change is required. This is a mindset and skill set that is never completely mastered but that, when done well, provides astonishing rewards!

Notes

1. Peter M. Senge, *The Fifth Discipline: The Art and Practice of The Learning Organization* (Doubleday/Currency, 1990).
2. Improvement work is also called kaizen; Improvements can be viewed as being either corrections to get back to standard or improvements to go beyond the current standard and achieve a new, higher level of performance.
3. First define strategic objectives and then determine the financial impact; Don't constrain your strategic intent and imagination with financial planning.
4. For a comprehensive study of strategy deployment, hoshin kanri, and the X-matrix, see Thomas L. Jackson, *Hoshin Kanri for the Lean Enterprise— Developing Competitive Capabilities and Managing Profit* (Productivity Press, 2006).
5. We say *messy* because it relies on open dialogue, strong communication, and solid Lead-with-Respect skills (see Chapter 2, "The Transformation Framework").
6. Peter Hines, Richard Lamming, Dan Jones, Paul Cousins, and Nick Rich, *Value Stream Management: Strategy and Excellence in the Supply Chain* (Upper Saddle River, NJ, Financial Times/Prentice Hall, 2000).

Chapter 11

Engineering Excellence

> We are what we repeatedly do. Excellence, then, is not an act, but a habit.
>
> **Aristotle**

Excellence Everywhere

In the preceding chapters, we developed the foundation of a lean system that quickly adapts to changing situations and continuously improves. This was made possible by the belief that better process leads to better results. Using process as the foundation for continuous improvement, rather than as a tool to blindly enforce consistency, creates an environment where experimentation and innovation can flourish. Mix in a focus on people and coaching, True North, and methodical problem solving, and you have the beginnings of a robust lean system. Ironically, even with this great start, lean IT implementations often overlook a critical component: technology. We refer to the application of lean to technology work as *engineering excellence*.

This book is not intended to be a technical manual; in this chapter we will not describe how to write better code or apply lean principles to enable efficient testing or best practices for cloud provisioning. Many other books already do a fine job in those realms. Rather, our message is intended to provide a framework to apply lean principles to the way work is done in your organization. That includes the technology work, not simply the processes on the periphery of the difficult and complex work of IT. The work of IT—developing and testing software, administering a database, provisioning a server, or any other technical task that is performed in your company—needs to be fused with your lean transformation.

As technologists, it is sometimes easier to think about lean as a means to improve the processes that enable the work of IT. Standup meetings, visual management, and other tools often focus on processes that facilitate technical tasks. Those are valuable things to focus on, but they are only part of the story. Creating a lean system of operational excellence in your organization mandates applying the principles and tools to all aspects of the work. Problem solving applies as much to fixing a slow page load for a website or selecting the appropriate technology for deploying infrastructure as it does to determining why there is a communication breakdown between the business and IT.

Antidogma

One of the challenges of writing about engineering excellence is the emotion it brings out in the technology community. Often practitioners are less inclined to find the right answer than they are to defend their choice of tool, methodology, or philosophy. Alistair Cockburn, an original signatory of the Agile Manifesto, created an "Oath of Non-Allegiance" in 2010:

> I promise not to exclude from consideration any idea based on its source, but to consider ideas across schools and heritages in order to find the ones that best suit the current situation. [1]

The basic premise of his oath is not getting caught up in the dogma of a particular school of thought so much that potentially useful ideas from elsewhere are dismissed without consideration. We see this flippant type of behavior consistently to this day. Battles in companies between traditional development (i.e., *waterfall*) proponents, tribal agilists, [2] and others rage in an ongoing struggle to guide the direction of the IT shop. The focus is often not on providing value to customers or other stakeholders, but rather on being right. This is not lean thinking (nor is it productive) and should be banished from your organization.

Many consultants and companies have made progress in attempting to bridge the gaps between different methodologies, practices, and philosophies. Through frameworks, certifications, and training seminars, connections and understanding have been built, but nothing has been able to completely stop the fighting (and likely never will; we are, after all, dealing with human emotion[3]). Perhaps the answer all along has been that there is no single answer, that the real value is in continuing to learn from one another and adapt to solve problems and progress. Lean thinking means keeping an inquisitive mind and openness to potential improvements in your processes, tools, and techniques. To think that any one body of knowledge has all the answers is unwise—as is dismissing all the work that has been done to date in improving the way we manage and deliver technology solutions. As a lean leader you are primarily a learner—learning both from what has been done by others and from your own experiments as you move forward with your transformation.

Similar to Alistair's oath, in this chapter we do not presuppose the use of any methodology, framework, or philosophy—be it agile or waterfall development, the IT Infrastructure Library (ITIL) for service management, DevOps, Scaled Agile Framework (SAFe[4]), or anything else. Lean can be used to move toward engineering excellence regardless of where you currently are. And the relentless pursuit of continuous improvement will lead you to where you need to go—whether that means breakthrough thinking and a completely new way of doing things or incremental changes to what you already have in place. The learning and discovery process is what matters, and we will help get you on the right path in the model line transformation.

Engineering Excellence in the Model Line

Let's look at how we can apply lean to help with some common technology problems such as the pace of technology change, keeping our employees' skills sharp, and problem solving.

Moving at Tech Speed

One thing is certain about working in technology: Nothing stays the same for very long. It wasn't so long ago when that wasn't the case. Anybody old enough (such as the authors!) remembers periods of relative stability within technology. Not anymore. Complex factors such as the exponential rise of computing power, the consumerization of IT, and breakthrough technologies have conspired to make keeping up with technical trends a challenge even for the most hard-core geeks. Children of today interact with computing power and technology that adults couldn't have dreamed of in their youth.

Instead of GI Joes and Matchbox cars, children today have smartphones and Minecraft. And the next generation of kids will have even more sophisticated and powerful toys.

It is not any different for adults in the workplace. Whether it's the latest programming language promising faster code creation with fewer defects, process and architectural innovations such as continuous delivery and two-speed IT,[5] or other trends such as mobile-first, big data, and cloud, technology in our workplaces is changing as fast as on the consumer side. And it is incredibly difficult to differentiate which of these changes requires the collective attention of the organization and which will fade away. But hopefully upon reading this book, you have acquired a new paradigm and some new tools in your lean tool kit that can help make sense of it all.

Technology Vision

In Chapter 10 we began to expand the use of lean, from being the way you operate and run your group day to day to the strategic system that governs mission and long-term planning. Using the principles of strategic alignment, you can ensure that the tactical daily focus of your group aligns to the strategy of the organization. For IT, this includes technology decisions and how to anticipate coming changes. Creating a robust strategy requires looking to the future to determine the types of skills your workforce will need. The discipline of strategic alignment creates an environment where your team is constantly asking the right questions, scanning the environment for coming changes, and preparing to act on opportunities.

Even with a great strategic alignment model, it is still not possible to predict the future. The real benefit of the system is the constant monitoring and scrutiny that allows for quick adaptation when the unexpected occurs. Creating an environment that aligns everyone to purpose infuses the organization with a greater ability to pivot and react quickly to change and take advantage of opportunities. Ensure as you deploy your strategic alignment system that technology strategy is included. Make the strategy visual in the organization and open it up to comments from the true tech experts—your frontline staff.

A3 Tech

The A3 tool is particularly well suited for representing the choices and changing environment of technology. Integrated into your strategic system or as a stand-alone work product, the A3 can also be used to articulate the complex world of technology, something we call a *technical A3*. Use it to document architectural decisions, tool selection, frameworks, platforms, etc. It creates not only a record of the choice and evolution of understanding, but also the factors that went into the decision and why the final choice was made. The beauty of the A3 is that it tells a story in such a way that it preserves organizational memory for future review, without the pain of reviewing arcane decision documents.

The technical A3 can also sometimes save us from ourselves! As IT professionals, we are occasionally prone to being wowed by the latest and greatest innovation. Often, technology is implemented simply because it can be, rather than because of a specific need, thus becoming a *solution in search of a problem*.[6] It's much easier to identify that this is happening when you have to answer the question, "What problem/opportunity are we addressing and what are we trying to accomplish here?" before purchasing or implementing new technology and tools.

Keeping Our Skills Sharp

In Chapter 9, we described the Teaching Thursdays program at Nationwide as a simple way to empower employees to take charge of getting the skills they need to be successful. It works because it's simple—the barriers to learning have been removed and the company makes the process fun and easy for the associates. Simplicity is a key factor in ensuring that your associates get the skills they need to be successful.

Simplicity is something many organizations overlook in trying to ensure that their workforces have been appropriately trained and are able to perform the functions of their jobs. We have seen it all—complex planning and forecasting tools, skills databases, learning platforms—and many fail miserably to do their primary job of identifying and helping associates get the skills they require. Without the ability to obtain new technical skills quickly, current associates are left out of consideration for new roles and, even worse, they are let go and replaced by someone in the market with the right skill set for that moment in time. Then the process repeats itself over and over, causing anguish for staff who are constantly worried about becoming obsolete and costing the company in repeatedly acquiring and onboarding new talent and showing the old guard the exit door.

To help ensure that your staff stay current with the skills they need to continue providing value to the organization, let's add a couple new features to your lean management system.

Visual Skills Matrix

The first feature is a Visual Skills Matrix, such as the example in Figure 11.1. The skills matrix is a visual representation of the skills your associates have, what they're working toward, and what skills the organization needs them to obtain. It is at the workgroup level—this is not a new HR system that attempts to gather the technology capabilities of everyone in your company. Most of the attempts we've seen to capture this type of information companywide have at best been useful for long-range forecasting, but never practical for tactical day-to-day operations. This visual is used as an additional accountability feature that ensures that members of the workforce have everything they need to be successful and, if not, that management focuses on providing the needed training, coaching, and resources.

The example in Figure 11.1 shows suggested elements that might work for your organization. There is a place for the current suite of technologies supported by your group, the technologies that are likely needed in the future, and a space for each person on the team along with what skills he or she needs, a target date, his or her current proficiency rating for each, and skills already attained. Also listed is whether or not there is a plan in place to acquire the new skills. While the associate is ultimately responsible for gaining the new knowledge, the manager has the accountability to ensure that the associate has the support and resources needed to accomplish the plan.

Visual skills matrix

Current skills: *Oracle DB, Java, CSS, HTML, Perl*

Needed skills: *Kony, Informatica, Ruby*

	Skills	Current level (1–5)	Needed level (1–5)	Date needed	Plan in place?
Praveen	*Java*	4	4	Done	Yes
	CSS	4	4	Done	Yes
	HTML	5	4	Done	Yes
	Kony	1	5	2/20	Yes
	Ruby	2	4	2/10	No
Mary	*Oracle DB*	4	3	Done	Yes
	Perl	5	3	Done	Yes
	Ruby	1	4	2/10	Yes

Figure 11.1   A Visual Skills Matrix example.

The Visual Skills Matrix works for all the same reasons as the other visuals you have implemented. It radiates information and calls people to action, it makes visible that which was previously hidden, and it creates a shared sense of accountability to complete what has been committed to.

Managers and associates share accountability for skill attainment. People must be willing to invest the energy to learn, and the manager must ensure that the opportunity is provided. Simply posting publicly that associates' skills are out of date is not in line with our repeated mantra of Respect for People. In fact, that would show *disrespect* toward the associates, because no mechanism to address the skills gap is included!

Cultural barriers may prove difficult when implementing this new component of your system. Human Resources might classify skills as confidential information, associates may view it as insulting to post what amounts to a virtual technology resume, and many of your managers may think that skill development is primarily the responsibility of the associates. Move swiftly to overcome these barriers. Just like the path you walked with making problems visible, make it safe to share openly what the skills profile of your group looks like.

Decouple skill profiles and your merit review process; focus on the improvement of individuals instead of their baseline. Which would you rather reward: the associate that comes with all the capabilities needed at a particular moment in time, but resists learning, or the associate who's willing to continue to sharpen his or her skills as the technology landscape changes? We'd take the learner over the knower any day of the week.

Standard Work for Learning

Like any visual board, the Visual Skills Matrix is of no value if it's not used and kept up to date. It must be supported with process and ultimately needs to guide behavior, helping management and staff provide value to stakeholders through the attainment of the right skills at the right time. For example, if your development team has not previously developed for mobile devices and does not have the know-how to do so, but you know that, in 2 months, everyone is expected to support a mobile-first development policy, change is needed to make sure that everyone is ready. Posting on the matrix the need for the skills, but not taking any action, is not going to produce results.

Luckily, you have already implemented a tool that is great for changing daily behavior: standard work. And through the introduction of strategy alignment, you should have a clear idea of where the company is heading and the tactics, skills, and resources necessary to get there. The next logical step is to introduce elements in both associate and leader standard work to ensure that skills acquisition and continuous learning are aligned to the technology strategy. Start with the new strategy review element in leader standard work: Where is the company heading and how does that impact your group and the skills needed? Use that information to regularly update the skills matrix.

Once you can see the information visually, it's time to plan how to develop the new skills. What action plans can you put in place for your associates? What coaching and support will they need? Do you need to supplement the current staff with new hires or contractors? Are there opportunities to pair staff in order to provide cross training and skill uplifts? Make sure an action plan is in place and agreed to by staff and management.

A3 Redux

The focus on learning and problem solving is what differentiates a lean leader. You are not implementing a methodology or a set of tools, but rather a full system that makes learning and new behaviors possible. You are not just optimizing the local team, or the workflow, or teaching your managers to be more effective; you are doing all of those things and more simultaneously. Effective lean transformations change the underlying culture of every aspect of the organization.

This type of culture change is not a natural phenomenon. It's not something that comes easily to organizations no matter how many times the phrase *problem-solving culture* is evoked by the management team. To create an environment that fosters problem solving, you have introduced the A3. The A3 process has been used in your transformation for problem solving, decision making, and updates to standard work. The processes surrounding the work product that encourage an experimental mindset, PDCA scientifically based problem solving, and consensus building are creating a foundation that will be very hard to shake once it's taken root.

Extend the use of the A3 to technical problem solving. If your company is like most, the A3 to this point has been used primarily for process changes and problems, but has been avoided for technical problems. Because the A3 does not prescribe a particular methodology for root cause problem solving, you have the freedom to implement what makes sense for you based on the complexity of the problem. You can get to the root cause of some technical problems through a simple 5 Whys inquiry; others will require more advanced analysis. In either case, the A3 gives you the flexibility to use the right analysis tools needed to bore to the appropriate level of understanding. And having a consistent method to frame, scope, and solve technical problems—one that enforces an understanding of the problem statement, current state, measurement, analysis, countermeasures, expected results, and check/adjust—is an incredible advantage.

The advantage of having a consistent way to frame and document technical problems also benefits general communication within the organization. IT staff often struggles with how to discuss complex problem resolution with internal customers and management. The A3 provides a straightforward method to make complex technical solutions clear and accessible to anyone. It also provides a methodical way to drive tool and technology decisions through the lens of objective criteria to evaluate alternative solutions (countermeasures) along with an easy way to tell the story of how the decisions were made.

Making the Commitment to Excellence

The journey to become a lean organization is not easy. That much should be clear as you progressed through this field guide. If you have been implementing the practices, tools, and principles we've covered, take the time to reflect if lean has been embedded in the technical work of your organization. While the lean journey never ends, your transformation is not complete if the core of your work—engineering excellence within IT—is not included.

Notes

1. http://alistair.cockburn.us/oath+of+non-allegiance.
2. *Tribal Agilist* is our term for people so caught up in proving the value of agile development over all other methods that they become what agile is fighting against: Rigid implementers of a framework and a process without consideration for the value they provide.
3. Rich Sheridan, author of *Joy, Inc.* (New York: Penguin Group, 2013), and CEO of Menlo Innovations, LLC, put it best during a conference presentation: "Conflict will always be there; we are, after all, dealing with humans—just salty bags of hormones."
4. http://www.scaledagileframework.com.

5. Bossert, O., Ip, C., and J. Laartz. *A Two Speed Architecture for the Digital Enterprise* (Insights and Publications, McKinsey&Company, 2014).
6. For a great discussion of this mental predisposition, see *Start by Diving Deep* by Jim Luckman and Durward Sobek, http://www.lean.org/LeanPost/Posting.cfm?LeanPostId=442.

Chapter 12

Continue the Journey

A journey is a person in itself; no two are alike. And all plans, safeguards, policing, and coercion are fruitless. We find that after years of struggle that we do not take a trip; a trip takes us.

John Steinbeck

It is fitting that we close our journey with a look back at the house we introduced at the beginning of this book (Figure 12.1). While it is impossible to predict all of the twists and turns of a transformation, the house provides a solid framework of a system designed to handle the challenges you'll certainly encounter. The journey you have chosen to undertake will never be complete; the mindset of a lean leader is one that stays hungry and focused on relentless improvement. Apply these principles and work systems to remove ambiguity and fear from the workplace and you will be amazed at the transformation! We hope you have begun your own journey in earnest and started to experience both the joy and struggle that come from such an endeavor.

This field guide can only take you so far. The real progress comes as you continue down the lean path with the humble intention to learn and adapt as you go. Take some comfort from knowing that you are not alone. Many others have walked this path before and are willing to help. Explore TheLeanITFieldGuide.com for more resources and support. We wish you the greatest success and lifelong learning!

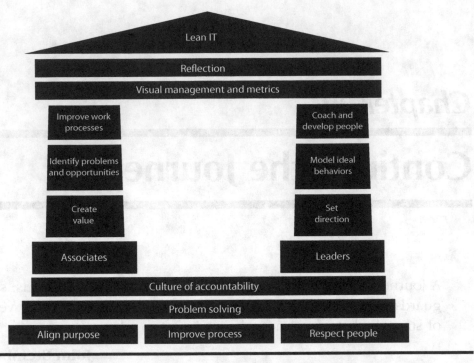

Figure 12.1   The lean IT house.

Index